Redemptive Intimacy

A New Perspective for the Journey to Adult Faith

Dick Westley

Loyola University of Chicago

TWENTY-THIRD PUBLICATIONS
P.O. Box 180 Mystic, CT 06355

ACKNOWLEDGMENTS

To have been given the opportunity to publicly "profess" one's faith can only be seen as a precious gift. I am sure that others may have used that gift better, but none with more gratitude.

My gratitude goes first to the members of my own base community, who by sharing their faith and their very lives with me brought me to see whatever of truth there is in this book. And secondly, to the Notre Dame Workshop Group, lovingly shepherded by Bill and Pat Reynolds and Father David Murphy, who have so graciously given me the chance to attempt to articulate that faith for the past 13 years. To both groups, I say that I repent that what you all have so generously shared with me was not better presented. I did the best I could.

I acknowledge my indebtedness to the authors and publishers of the works cited in this book and listed in the bibliography.

Special thanks are due to Pat Kluepfel and John van Bemmel of Twenty-Third Publications for their patience with me in bringing this work to completion, and for their expert and wise counsel which made it better than it otherwise would have been.

Dick Westley
July, 1980

ISBN 0-89622-123-7

Library of Congress Catalog Card No. 80-54810

Edited by Marie McIntyre
Cover design by SAK Group
Book design by John G. van Bemmel

DEDICATION

People can't believe in anything but incarnation. Incarnation means more than that Jesus is both God and man. It also means that God is incarnate not only in Jesus, but in *our* history and in *our* very flesh.

The Lord dwells not in images, laws, or rituals; not in Jerusalem, Mecca, or even Rome—but in people—in our noblest parts where justice and charity dwell.

In Loving Memory of My Father

JOHN FRANCIS WESTLEY

June 24, 1903 - May 12, 1980

The most loving Christian I have ever known, who by incarnating the highest ideals of this book made God real for me, and brought me to know what it means to say of God—he is *our Father*.

CONTENTS

Dick Westley's *Redemptive Intimacy* comes at the right time. Religious people are realizing the importance of small communities for creative living. *Redemptive Intimacy* came out of small group experiences and is designed to facilitate and be a resource for them. But this book is not the usual bland and pious fare that group discussion books are prone to be. It is at one and the same time the story of Dick Westley's own journey and an invitation to others to explore their own story.

Redemptive Intimacy is a feisty book that attacks and defends, not in a gratuitously polemical way, but out of a passion for life and a concern for redemption. This book will get things going and keep them going. It is a strong statement about the relationship between faith and life.

Rev. John Shea
Saint Mary of the Lake Seminary
Mundelein, Illinois

Introduction

Experience Is Revelatory

The central theme of this book is that for Christians redemption and intimacy are really one and the same. I claim no originality for that thought because I believe its truth is readily available to Christians who give heed to their faith and experience, and are fortunate enough to live long enough. I have lived long enough to see the day when the truth about the identity of redemption and intimacy finally dawned upon me. Now I feel called upon to share this insight.

If you are one of those people who is content with the way we have been telling the Christian Story, if nothing in your experience gives you reason to yearn for a new and more appropriate language with which to give a contemporary profession of faith, then you may be among those who will find this book troublesome.

If on the other hand you have found that the only language available to you for speaking in faith to co-believers somehow does violence to your own experience of the Lord, or if you are somewhat embarrassed by the rather simplistic and childish way you continue in adult life to speak of faith to your children, who find what you say about God and Church totally unbelievable, then you have had some of the same experiences I have, and will find this book helpful.

Let me candidly admit that there are two basic assumptions I have taken for granted in what follows. Though I offer no proof for them, I am convinced that to deny them is to turn away from the light. The first assumption is that *experience is revelatory.* Authentic human experiences have a way of illuminating and transforming one's faith about God and the Church. This is because God is constantly at work revealing himself to us in everyday experiences. Theologians and preachers not in touch with those revelatory dimensions of human life address us at their own risk. For what they say will invariably be unmasked as hollow, as abstract, not validated by experience, and hence erroneous. Nor does an ecclesiastical office exempt one from the task of being in touch with what the Spirit is presently revealing to the People of God in their experiences. Not even the inspired writers of the Scriptures are above this process of experiential validation, as becomes immediately clear when one reflects upon St. Paul's view of marriage and of women as given in I Corinthians 7 and elsewhere. *It is communally funded experience that should shape our theology, not theology our experience.* This is an extremely important point.

The second assumption follows from the first. If God is revealing himself to us in our experience, then it is essential for us believers to take the time and have the institutional mechanisms for gathering to share and get in touch with that experience. Since it is not *my* individual experiences or *yours* which are revelatory, we must evaluate our own experiences in the light of what the Spirit is revealing to the Church, the People of God, first in the lives of those with whom we immediately share our faith and eventually *with all believers.* Whenever a truth is validated by the experiences of believers in many regions or countries, we may say it is "communally funded" and that it begins to approach what theologians call the *sensus fidelium,* the consensus of believing people. Such consensus has been traditionally recognized as an authentic source of revelation, but in recent times it has not been taken seriously enough by ecclesiastical authorities. So my second assumption is: *Dialogue, faith sharing, and experience sharing in the name of the Lord are an essential work of the People of God.*

As practical Americans, we tend to think that all groupings of believers aside from liturgy should be action-oriented. People gather to do something together which they could not do alone. We know that we are called by the Gospel to social action, yet there is something Pope Pius XII once called "the heresy of action." By this, he meant that we must also understand that we are called not only to "do" something, but also to "be" something, or better "to be the Lord together." Our doing must flow from our being. When we devote all of our time to the doing, eventually we burn out, we run down, we find ourselves finally unable to do any longer. The life of Christian doing can only be sustained by faith and a deep spirituality, so some time must be devoted as well to the cultivation of those things.

In view of these two assumptions, I would not be so bold

as to claim that what I say in this book is true. That is not for me to say. But I do claim that I know how to find out whether what I am proclaiming about *redemptive intimacy* is true or not. To verify what I say, it is necessary to share it with the believing and Spirit-filled People of God. If what I say is corroborated by *their* faith and experience, then it will be true, as true as any theological account can ever be.

Ideally then, this book should not be read alone, as if it were simply a textbook in theoretical theology. It has been written with a deep conviction about the importance of experience, and the absolute necessity of all of us sharing our faith and experiences with one another. The book will most certainly be of less value than its author had hoped if it does not become the occasion for small groups of Christians/Catholics to gather for that purpose. What is said in this book is not nearly as important as the sharing, that is *redemptive intimacy,* which it is intended to precipitate and, I hope, facilitate.

To that end, each chapter is divided into several smaller sections, each of which can be used as the basis for a dialogue session. Questions aimed at helping the group get into the sharing process can be found at the end of this book. Since I have been a member of such a base community within my parish for the past nine years, much of what I have learned about redemptive intimacy I owe to the members of that community. And as a member of such a faith-sharing group, I know firsthand how important it can be to have some sort of material available to get the dialogue started each meeting.

Those interested in using this book as a tool for small group dialogue may find it helpful to consult the appendix entitled, *Building a Household Church.* Some of the basic principles governing dialogue and faith sharing that our group has discovered are shared there. In fact, if you are fortunate enough to have a group of believers with whom to dialogue about the material in this book, it is suggested that your first meeting (or meetings—it may take more than one) be devoted to coming to grips with what is said in that appendix.

What is said there should not be taken as normative. There is no one way to proceed; you must let your experience be your guide. On the other hand, if you are alone with no believers with whom to dialogue, this book might be a good way for you to take the initiative of starting such a group. Usually, in every parish or neighborhood, there are those who are starving for dialogue and faith sharing and they will eagerly respond if you but put out the call.

Finally, this book is primarily concerned with presenting the theological hypothesis that *intimacy is redemptive*. To simply assert that out of the blue, however, would not prove helpful to you. In my own life, I only came to accept that hypothesis as inevitable after a somewhat involved process of spiritual development. For the sake of greater clarity and in order to avoid unnecessary misunderstandings, I have thought it best to devote Chapters One and Two to an account of the essential elements and moves of the spiritual journey that finally brought me to the point where I could accept what my experience had been trying to reveal to me all along.

Chapters Three to Six are devoted to a consideration of certain basic truths which, when accepted, allow the truth about intimacy to come into view. Chapter Seven, from which the book takes its title, is a direct statement of the redemptive intimacy hypothesis. Chapters Eight and Nine present some of the consequences that follow from all this for Christian life and spirituality.

For those who are disappointed that this entire book is not devoted to the topic of "intimacy," let me mention two books that are. I recommend them to anyone interested in that topic. In fact, as I look back on the matter, I realize that I received much from each of them and would see my book as merely adding a "theological" or "faith" perspective to the precious truths found within their pages. Those books are: *The Miracle of Dialogue* by Reuel L. Howe (Seabury Press, New York, 1963); and *On Caring* by Milton Mayeroff (Harper & Row, New York, 1971).

CHAPTER ONE

Tracing the Beginnings of the Journey

It has been said that even the longest journey begins with the first step. I have searched my heart and memory to discover just when it was I took my first decisive step toward what I have come to call a theology of *redemptive intimacy*. Despite my best efforts, I have been unable to identify a specific moment that marks the beginning of my personal journey and search. Instead, it seems to have been a series of significant moves over a period of years that finally shattered my complacency with the *status quo* and started me down the road to my present state of mind. What gives unity to those disparate moments in my life and allows me to call them a ''beginning'' is the fact that they all had to do with my understanding of the meaning and significance of Church in human life.

Though I did not recognize it at the time, when I began to see new meaning and significance in the fact that in my own life, I had been moving from one vision of the Church to another. I was beginning a journey that would ultimately cause me to call into question the traditional way of telling the Christian Story. It is not any particular vision of the Church which marks the beginning of that journey, but rather the insight into the meaning of the movement itself from one vision of Church to another. In this chapter, I shall try to give an accurate account of that movement and of the insight it generated, because to the best of my knowledge that is how it all began for me.

Throughout the history of the Church, whenever Catholic people have found their faith particularly meaningful and have lived the Christian life with joy and enthusiasm, it has always been in response to the Good News of the Gospel *and* a particular vision of Church. A vision of Church that not only gave believable answers to questions like: What is Church? or Why be a Catholic?, but also was so moving and powerful as to generate the kind of energy and enthusiasm that has always characterized us Catholics at our best. It is hard to overestimate the importance of such visions because what a people take the Good News of the Gospel to be is itself a function of their vision of Church.

There are those who would say that all that is needed for a vital Christian life is the Bible, and all else is superfluous. I strongly disagree with that assessment, and for the following reason. If we say that the Gospel is "Good News," how can we tell them what in it is "Good News" and what isn't? What we take to be the "Good News" dimension of Scripture is a function of our vision of what the Christian enterprise is really all about. When we come to the book with that sort of perspective, then things fall into place. We can then say that this is central and that is peripheral. But when we approach the Bible without such a perspective, it seems more like a confusing Tower of Babel than divine revelation. Of course, when we approach the book from differing perspectives, we end up with different versions of the "Good News."

Part of the fragmentation among Catholics is due to the fact that, at present, there is no agreement on that crucial perspective, the meaning and significance of Church. The Catholic community is currently strung out across three different but related visions of Church, i.e., as *Bark,* as *Body,* or as *Sign.* As a middle-aged Catholic, I find that at one time or another in my life I actually held each of the three models or visions before moving on to that view of Church which constitutes an integral part of my "redemptive intimacy" theology.

A View of the Church as the Bark of Salvation

Like most in my age group who attended Catholic schools as youngsters, I was raised on and indoctrinated in a view of Church as *the* Bark of Salvation. The primary goal, we were told, was "saving our souls." And to accomplish that, we had to avoid sin and be particularly careful to be sure we died in the state of grace. The Church had been instituted, so the story went, to be of assistance to us in that vital work of salvation. The Church possessed all the necessary means of salvation, and so was itself necessary for salvation. Separation from the Church put one's salvation in question and hence it was a foolhardy move for one to initiate. To be forced out was considered the severest of ecclesiastical punishments. To our young minds, then, separation from the Church was tantamount to damnation. Conversely, we had the clear impression that if we did but remain good practicing Catholics, our own salvation was practically assured.

More specifically, the scenario presented went something like this:

Adam and Eve sinned and the gates of heaven were closed to men. But despite the fall, God did not abandon man, whom he had made. Rather he promised a Redeemer, one who would re-open the gates of heaven and initiate a new and eternal plan of salvation for the human race. God so loved the world that he sent as our Redeemer, his only begotten Son. Jesus Christ, the Son of God made flesh, died a bloody death on the cross to redeem us from our sins. He founded a Church which was to play the essential role in the new and eternal convenant he established between God and the human race.

It became commonly understood that *extra ecclesiam nemo salvatur,* that is, "outside the Church no one can be saved." And if one were to ask why this is so, it would be easy to reply that the Church has been made the guardian, custodian and dispenser of the necessary means of salvation. After all, the Lord did say to Nicodemus that "Unless a man be born again of water and the Holy Spirit he cannot enter into the Kingdom of Heaven" (John 3:5). And to the Jews he had said: "Unless a man eat my flesh and drink my blood he cannot have life in him" (John 6:54–55).

The meaning is clear: Baptism and Eucharist are *in some way* necessary for salvation, and these and the other Sacraments have been put in the keeping of the Church. Consequently, in a real sense the Church is herself necessary for salvation as well.

This way of viewing the situation constitutes what I am calling the "Bark of Salvation" view of the Church. Catholics could not help compare themselves to Noah of the Old Testament. The similarities were strikingly clear. Just as all who were not on board the original ark perished in the flood, so all those not joined to Christ in the safe sanctuary of the Catholic Church perish in the perilous seas through which the Bark of Peter carefully makes its way toward salvation.

So it was that every precaution was taken to insure that we Catholics were as much as possible kept apart from pagans (non-believers), those of other Christian denominations, and those of other religions. The lengths to which those in charge would go in order to insure that separation are evident in two stories from my grade school days.

I recall coming to school one morning only to be met by a nun at the door with her poised index finger up to her lips signalling absolute silence to all who entered. We were told to go directly to our classrooms and to be still. Monsignor Traudt, the pastor, was having a conference with the principal in her office. In those days, that was a major and somewhat ominous event. Something important was afoot, but what?

We learned later that the conference was to determine the dismissal time each day for the school. The presence of Monsignor was all the proof anyone needed that the decision was viewed as a ''pastoral'' one, having to do with the ''care of souls.'' It turned out that the point at issue in that Milwaukee grade school that Fall morning in 1939 centered around the fact that the public schools in the area were being dismissed each day at 3:30 in the afternoon. This meant that each school day at that hour the neighborhood streets were filled with pagan and Protestant children, so something had to be done to avoid unnecessary contact between them and the good children of St. Anne's. I have always been grateful to Monsignor for his sensitivity. He decided that if we were dismissed at 3:10 we could be safely behind the doors of our Catholic homes at the bewitching hour of 3:30 P.M. (I never would have forgiven him had he gone the other way and kept us in school each day until 4:00!)

A year later, I was almost expelled from St. Anne's when Monsignor learned that I had gone swimming at the YMCA pool in our area. That was putting oneself in an unnecessary relation with non-Catholic Christians and was therefore an occasion of sin. He relented only because it was clear that in my innocence I hadn't known of the gravity of what I had done. But of course I was warned never to do it again. I never have. Monsignor died shortly thereafter, and it has been years since I gave up the Bark of Salvation view of the Church, but to this day whenever I drive past a YMCA, I still feel distant echoes of the guilt-trip he laid on me back in 1940. That was 40 years ago! Who says that experiences of our youth don't leave indelible marks on our adult life for good or ill?

It is easy enough for us in the post-Vatican II era to smile at such goings on, but the salvation game was played with deadly seriousness in those days and it was no laughing matter. Many of my classmates from those years who were children of mixed marriages suffered excruciating pain from the fact that, in the prevailing view of Church, they were being asked to perceive their non-Catholic parent as in grave and present danger of damnation unless he or she converted. This put my classmates under the burdensome obligation to work unceasingly for the conversion of their non-Catholic parents. Such families were subjected to extreme pressures to not attend weddings, funerals, etc. even of family members when they were held in other than Catholic churches. Catholics were not to fraternize with non-Catholics, and if that caused inhuman pain to mixed-marriage families, that was an additional sign of why such marriages were to be avoided at all costs.

The lengths to which a local Church was prepared to go in this regard can be seen in a final story from my youth. Archbishop Samuel Stritch, a beloved and gentle man who later became the Cardinal Archbishop of Chicago, was then Archbishop of Milwaukee. In a move by no means typical of this loving man, he startled the Catholic population of Milwaukee by announcing that all those who had their children in public schools would henceforth be denied absolution in confession. Now while that may appear to be a harsh and unfeeling move to us in retrospect, it is the only logical move to make if one holds that the Catholic Church is the Bark of Salvation. Fraternization could only lead to more mixed marriages, and mixed marriages were a scourge on the Catholic community that had to be stamped out.

It was in such a climate of separatism that I spent my formative years in the Catholic Church. But I was not only separated from my non-Catholic neighbors, I was also made to feel separate from the clergy and religious within the Church. Since the Church was in the "salvation business," it had been entrusted with the Mass and the Sacraments which were the necessary means of salvation. But the majority of Catholics were simply called upon to be willing but passive recipients of the means of salvation and to be docile passengers on the Bark of Peter, obedient to the directives of the captain and crew.

The clergy and religious were the real movers and shakers in this salvation drama, because it was through them that the means of salvation were made available to the rest of us. Archbishop Stritch and Monsignor Traudt could, and did, make their presence felt in every Catholic home in their respective jurisdictions. Nor was that thought to be inappropriate; it was what we expected from the clergy because we all shared the same vision of Church and fully understood that "salvation" was the name of the game. There may have been grumbling now and then, but there was never any real dissent voiced, at least not in front of the children.

So long as I was young and made no attempt to think for myself or evaluate the Bark of Salvation view in terms of my own experience, I was quite comfortable. And why shouldn't I have been? After all, I was "in" the Bark, and so had nothing to be afraid of except myself, for I was always capable of not living up to the standards of faith I espoused. But from the start I took what I was taught very seriously, and cannot ever remember a time in my life when I was not really trying to live up to the vision of Church I held. Yet despite all this good will, as I moved on to high school, I had a feeling that there was something very wrong with the view of Church I had been given, but I couldn't put my finger on what it was. Obviously, I was ripe for a new and different scenario about the meaning of Church. Thankfully, I didn't have long to wait.

A View of the Church as the Body of Christ

I began high school in 1942, and the very next year great impetus was given to one of St. Paul's favorite images of the Church, when Pope Pius XII issued his great and rightly famous encyclical, *On The Mystical Body of Christ*. The impact was immediate and electric, and for myself I am sure it accounted for the fact that during my last three years in high school, my religion/theology classes were the most exciting and meaningful in my schedule.

St. Paul had often spoken of the Church as the "Body of Christ"; we were the members and Christ was the Head. (See Rom. 12:4 ff.; 1 Cor. 12:12 ff.; Eph. 1:23, 4:12 ff., 5:23; Col. 1:18, 2:19, and 3:15.) Pius XII's encyclical was an attempt to give a contemporary expression to this very traditional view. The encyclical was released at the height of World War II, when the Germans were at the gates of Rome and the Pope's fate was very much in doubt. It can and should be read, therefore, as Pius XII's last will and testament to the Catholic people. The fact that he survived and reigned gloriously for many more years in no way changes that evaluation, first because of the greatness of the document, and second because Pius did not know at the time that he would survive and be allowed to rule the Church. As spiritual father to the Catholics on both sides of the conflagration, the war was a real anguish for him. His encyclical was written to help them realize what it meant to be members of Christ's Body and what a scandal it was for them to be at war with one another.

Looking back on the situation, it can be said that the vision of Church which was presented in that encyclical became the most powerful and dynamic view among Catholics for the next 20 years, from 1943 to 1963, or until the time of Vatican II. A key reason for its popularity was the fact that it delineated an important role in the Church for laymen and laywomen, even the fathers and mothers of families. They were no longer to be looked on merely as the precious cargo of the Bark, but were called upon to be active co-redeemers with Christ in the salvation of the whole world. The terribly low estate of the laity in those days can be judged from the fact that Pius XII felt obliged to write in *On The Mystical Body* (17):

> Let this be clearly understood, especially in these our days: fathers and mothers of families . . . occupy an honorable . . . place in the Christian community, and even they, under the impulse of God and with His help, can reach the heights of supreme holiness, which Jesus Christ has promised will never be wanting to the Church.

When the history of the 20th century Catholicism is written, this great encyclical of Pius XII, will be seen to have marked the beginning of a new era in the Catholic Church, and to have been a call in faith for non-celibate Catholics to assume their rightful roles in the Lord's own work. Pope John XXIII and his Vatican Council II built so well on this initiative of Pius XII that ours is being called "The Age of the Laity." So for 20 years, this vision of Church was responsible for a renewed vitality of faith in those of us who accepted it. Of course, the majority of Catholics continued to hold on to the old Bark of Salvation view, but the young were being schooled in the Body of Christ view. It was that vision of Church which generated the tremendous Catholic Action movement which gave us such things as: the Christian Family Movement (CFM), Cana, Young Christian Students (YCS), and Young Christian Workers (YCW), etc. If one doubts how important is the vision of Church that one has, she need only recall the excitement and power generated by the vision of the Church as the Body of Christ, the last unifying vision to energize the Catholic people.

As a high school student, I was fortunate enough to have been exposed to the new vision of Church, and so when I went off to college. I remember joining a Catholic Action group that ran a sports program and taught religion to adolescent boys in the State reform schools. I continued to grow in my knowledge and appreciation of the Church as the Body of Christ in my college theology classes, and was fortunate enough to have had an immediate opportunity to share what I was learning with others. That proved to be a forecast of things to come.

Once out of college, I devoted the next four years to my graduate work and to making a good beginning in my new marriage, all the while being spiritually sustained by the new vision of Church. When my graduate work was completed, Ethel and I joined a CFM group and once again got into the dynamic of living the Body of Christ theology in a Catholic Action group. As a college teacher, I was given many opportunities to work with young people all over the country, giving weekend workshops on the theology of the Mystical Body in high schools from coast to coast. I enjoyed every minute of it, and would have to confess that I remain a Mystical Body Catholic in my heart. Even though my head has moved on, to this day if you scratch me, up bubbles the old Body of Christ theology. What precisely was it? Why was it so effective? And how was it an improvement over the Bark of Salvation view?

In the Bark of Salvation view of the Church, the centrality and necessity of the Church was seen to lie in the fact that only those *in* the Bark of Peter were saved. *Outside* the Church salvation was not possible. The Body of Christ view continues to hold that the Church is necessary for salvation, but it sees that necessity differently. Instead of saying that "outside" the Church there is no salvation, it says that "without" the Church there is no salvation, *sine ecclesia nemo salvatur.* That seems to be such a little change, but in reality it is monumental. For to say that there is no salvation outside the Church, is to say that one must be a Roman Catholic to be saved. To say that there is no salvation "without" the Church, is to say that wherever salvation occurs, be it inside or outside the Church, it can only happen *through* the Church.

The new scenario might read something like this:

Christ came to win the graces necessary for the salvation of all. By his life, death, resurrection, and ascension, Christ opened the gates of heaven and won sufficient graces for all of humankind to be saved. He is thus Savior of the whole world. But when those graces of redemption come to be distributed to souls, the Lord God has chosen to put himself in need of us. Pius XII put it this way (*On The Mystical Body,* 44, 12):

> . . . Yet this also must be held, marvellous though it may seem: Christ has need of His members. This is not because He is indigent and weak, but rather because He has so willed it for the greater glory of His spotless Spouse. Dying on the cross, He (Christ) left to His Church the immense treasury of redemption toward which she (the Church) contributed nothing. But when those graces come to be distributed not only does Christ share this work of sanctification with His Church, but He wills that in some way it be due to her action. This is a deep mystery, and an inexhaustible subject of meditation, that the salvation of many depends on . . . the members of the Mystical Body of Jesus Christ. . . . It was possible for Christ of Himself to impart these graces to mankind directly; *but he has willed to do so only through a visible Church made up of men so that through her all might cooperate with Him in dispensing the graces of redemption.*

Metaphorically, we might say that the infinite merits of the redemption are stored in an immense reservoir, but a reservoir with no outlets. To supply outlets for redemptive grace to all of humankind within and outside the Church is precisely why Christ founded the Church. Each Catholic is to make of her life an outlet of saving grace for others, the size or caliber of the outlet depends directly on the qualitative way she lives the Christian life.

What a marked contrast from the preceding view! Even after all these years, I can still feel the urgency, the energy, and the power that emanate from that account of the Christian enterprise. I continue to be moved by it, and shall never fully understand why a lay Catholic would prefer remaining in the old Bark of Salvation to becoming an active co-worker with Christ in the salvation of the world. It has become fashionable these days to speak of empowerment, yet I know of no single ecclesiastical document as empowering of the faithful as Pius XII's 1943 encyclical, written 20 years before the start of Vatican II.

In one of his many books from the period, Thomas Merton gave a beautiful and concrete account of how this Body of Christ theology works. I shall never forget the account, though I must confess to having been unable to remember in which of his books it occurs. It is such a helpful account, that even though I am unable to quote it *verbatim,* let me share it with you in my own words.

Merton has insomnia, which is really a trial in the life of a Trappist. You are awakened for choir at 2:00 A.M., but when you return you cannot go back to sleep. You lie there listening to the monk in the cell to the right of you begin to snore and fall asleep, and likewise with the monk to the left of you, without yourself being able to sleep. In addition, the tower clock tolls every 15 minutes, thus keeping you perfectly informed as to just how much sleep you are missing. Reflecting on his predicament, Merton gives a stirring account of the Body of Christ in action.

You lie there, inert and helpless, crushed by the inscrutable tyranny of time, not knowing why you are a victim. But somewhere out in the world where it is night, someone is finally able to see that what he has been doing is terribly wrong and at long last finds himself able to repent.

The point is crystal clear. Thomas Merton, a Trappist monk shut off from the world, joins his sufferings with those of Christ, thus making of his life an outlet of grace. Half way across the world, someone whom he does not know and whom he has never met feels the power of God's grace in his life and turns from his evil ways. Alone, in the dark in his monastery, Merton has become a channel of grace for others. *That* is the Body of Christ in action, and that is the co-redemptive work to which not only priests and religious are called but to which each and every member of the Church is also called. No wonder the watchword of the day was ''Offer it up!'' You may well have difficulties and pains to contend with, but there is a world out there that is in desperate need of grace, so don't waste that pain and sorrow; put it to redemptive use for others.

Unfortunately, the moving ''Body of Christ'' account of the Christian enterprise was not without its own difficulties. For in addition to articulating that inspiring theology, Pius XII went on to lay down certain conditions that had to be met before one's life could be co-redemptive with Christ's. In the most troublesome and controversial remark of the entire encyclical, he said (22):

> Actually only those are to be included as members of the Church who have been baptized with water and profess the true faith, and who have not been so unfortunate as to separate themselves from the unity of the Body or to have been excluded by lawful authority.

So it would seem that only those who meet those three conditions are bonafide members of the Body of Christ and hence co-redeemers with him in the salvation of the world. But that means that only Roman Catholics can be outlets of saving grace to the world. All others can only be on the receiving end of the actions of the Body of Christ, and regardless of the quality of their spiritual lives they can never become truly co-redemptive.

In the end, the bottom line in this account is that though there is indeed salvation outside the Catholic Church, the Church remains necessary for the salvation of all because in accord with the will of God only its members can be channels of saving grace. To be sure, the Church also teaches that God has promised that his grace will always be available in such strength as to be sufficient for all. But that is interpreted to mean that he will see to it that there are always sufficient numbers of Catholics leading co-redemptive lives at any given moment to insure the availability of sufficient grace for all. It could not be otherwise, since according to this theology every grace coming into the world is channeled through the bonafide members of Christ's Body, i.e., through Roman Catholics. It is through the co-redemptive lives of its members, then, that the Catholic Church is the mediatrix of all grace.

The main reason for being, becoming, or remaining a Catholic then is not in order to be saved—one need not be a Catholic for that to happen—but rather in order to become, with Christ, a co-redeemer in the salvation of the world.

This view of the Church as the Body of Christ was such a welcome improvement over the rather stifling Bark of Salvation view, that at first I noticed only that fact. The Bark of Salvation view was so self-centered as to be inauthentically Christian; after all, Jesus was the man for others. At least in the Body of Christ view that dimension of being "for others" was paramount. But as time wore on, I became more and more ill at ease about that view. I wasn't sure I really believed that God never conferred grace on anyone directly without mediation.

Then too, there was that troublesome section 22. In my work with young people, I presented only the positive parts of the theology of the Body of Christ and tried to avoid getting into the problem of who was or who was not a bonafide member. So after almost two decades of total commitment to this view, the feeling of dissatisfaction that had once before signaled that it was time for me to give up the Bark of Salvation view began to reappear. Evidently, it was once again time to move on. And as before, an event in the universal Church showed me the direction, for on October 11th, 1962 John XXIII convened Vatican Council II, the twenty-first general or ecumenical council of the Roman Catholic Church.

A View of the Church as the People of God and Sacrament of Salvation

Almost immediately after the appearance of the encyclical on *The Mystical Body* in 1943, a theological disagreement arose concerning membership in the Body of Christ. The dialogue and discussion among the theologians on this problem at times became heated, but finally it was generally agreed that section 22 of that document had been much too restrictive. A desire to open up bonafide membership to all Christians began to surface, and so it was no surprise to find Vatican II doing just that. In fact, the Council Fathers found the topic of the nature of the Church so important that they devoted not one but two documents specifically to it, the dogmatic *Constitution on the Church* (COC) and the pastoral *Constitution on the Church in the Modern World* (CMW).

A reading of those documents clearly indicates that in presenting the Vatican II view of the Church, the Council Fathers had Pius XII very much in mind. To those who had in the preceding 20 years become acquainted with the Body of Christ view of the Church, the teaching of Vatican II seemed not so much new and revolutionary as the logical next step in our ongoing and developing understanding of Church. Unfortunately, the majority of Catholics had never adopted the Body of Christ perspective, remaining firmly rooted in the Bark of Salvation view. To them, the Vatican II view seemed not only revolutionary, but even unorthodox. For such Catholics, Vatican II was a betrayal and a source of much pain and bitterness. In all probability, it may very well not have been possible for them to make sense of the current developments in our self-understanding of Church without first going back to pick up a real understanding of the Body of Christ view.

The essentials of the Vatican II scenario on the nature and significance of the Church in the Christian enterprise are as follows:

God at all times and among *every* people, has given welcome to whosoever acknowledges him and does what is right, but he had willed to save humankind by making them into a single people (COC 9). For just as the Jewish nation was the "people of God" in the Old Testament, so in the new and eternal testament there is to be a special people formed by Christ for the salvation of the world.

This special people is God's chosen instrument of salvation and made up of those who: a) have been baptized; b) believe in Christ and accept him as their head; c) have the Holy Spirit dwelling in a special way within them; and who d) live their lives according to the law of love (COC 9).

Though a minority of the total population of the earth at any given time, this people constituted by Christ are the hope and instrument of salvation for all of humankind. And if one were to attempt to describe the nature of this instrument of salvation, she would have to say it is a "Sacrament." For if a Sacrament is an outward sign instituted by Christ to give grace, this is precisely what the People of God are. The Church as the People of God is *the* Sacrament of Salvation, because the Church simultaneously manifests and exercises the mystery of God's salvific love for all people. (CMW 45).

Having obviously described the People of God in such a way as to include all Christians and not just Catholics, the Council Fathers felt obliged to say something specifically about Catholics (COC 14);

> Catholics are the privileged of the privileged. They alone of the People of God are *fully* incorporated into Christ in ways which other Christians are not. Full incorporation into Christ requires that one: a) possess the Spirit of Christ; b) accept the entire system and means of salvation (Mass and the Seven Sacraments); c) be joined to that structure which Christ rules through the pope and bishops; and d) persevere in Christian charity in everyday life.

And then as if to insure that no misunderstanding would occur, they added (COC 14):

> The Church is necessary for salvation, and whoever knows that the Catholic Church was made necessary for salvation and still refuses to enter her cannot be saved.

For those of us who had been energized and empowered by the Body of Christ view of the matter, the Vatican II version was something of a disappointment. It lacked the sort of charism that comes from courageously moving out in accord with a prophetic vision grounded in communally funded faith experiences. It seemed uncertain, unwilling to abandon fully and once and for all the primitive Bark of Salvation view. That uncertainty has led to debilitating ambiguities and prevented the Council from coming up with a dynamic vision of Church to replace the Body of Christ view. By opting to attempt a compromise between the Bark of Salvation and Body of Christ views, it has left the challenge of how to follow the Spirit into the future largely unanswered, and has therefore plunged the Church into dark confusion.

It goes without saying that I was personally left in a kind of limbo by the Vatican II view. I had been so ready to make the next move in my spiritual journey, only to find myself forced into a holding pattern. True, Vatican II had affirmed non-Catholic Christians in ways unheard of before, just as the Body of Christ view before it had affirmed the laity. But that benefit was overshadowed by an obvious retreat to the Bark of Salvation mentality at key junctures in Vatican II documents. For a time I was gravely disappointed. But my original dissatisfaction slowly gave way to wonder, as I began to realize something important. The Bark of Salvation view has been on the scene for centuries; the Body of Christ view had been dynamic and vital for only 20 years. Here it was five years after Vatican II, and already that view of Church was seen by growing numbers as interim, inadequate, and as a prelude to something bigger.

After centuries of thinking that there was only one acceptable view of the Church, Catholics were being taught a vital lesson by the Spirit, as the lifetime of each new vision of the Church became shorter and the pace of the change from vision to vision accelerated. What was important about Vatican II was not the view of Church it presented, so much as the fact that the view it bequeathed us was unable to retain its vitality for more than several years. *Vatican II was not the last word at all; it was the exciting prelude to something more.* If only I could discern what that more was, I might be able to plot the direction the Spirit was giving the Christian enterprise in our day. What was the hidden lesson to be learned from all that I had been through?

The Lesson To Be Learned

One thing that all three views we considered have in common is that each insists that the Church, however it was defined, is in some way necessary for salvation. Yet the development from one view to the other seems to indicate that if that is truly the case, we have yet to give it an acceptable verbal expression. There is a growing uneasiness about claiming that the institutional Church is necessary for salvation because that seems to infringe on the freedom of God. We seem to be limiting God by insisting that he effect the salvation of humankind through the Church. And it doesn't help matters much to insist that God has freely willed it that way, because the communally funded experience of many is that though God sometimes works through the Church, he doesn't do so always. Given that experience, the question bothering us today, put bluntly, is whether the Catholic Church is necessary for salvation in any way at all.

The Church was important and essential in the Bark of Salvation view because no one outside the Church could be saved. In the Body of Christ and People of God views, the Church was necessary for salvation because only its members could be said to be instruments in the work of redemption, though in each of these views membership was looked at differently. In the Body of Christ view it was restricted to Catholics, in the People of God view it was restricted to Christians. Would we not, perhaps, have a more acceptable view of how God works in the world if only we refrained from insisting either that the Catholic Church is necessary for salvation, or that Christians are the source of salvation to non-Christians?

What would such a more humble view of the Church look like? And if the Church is not in the salvation business, what is its importance? Why did Christ found the Church if not to be the source of salvation?

To answer those questions, it is necessary to propose a new scenario:

Christ came to reveal to humankind that God is the loving Father of all, and that the gift of his salvation is ready to hand. It is assumed that as loving Father, God is constantly at work in every human life, drawing us ever closer to himself by means of the Spirit. Humans find it difficult to accept this fact and to recognize the hand of God in their midst. So the Father sent his Son to found a Church which would be a special, identifiable group among whom the Spirit of God worked manifestly and openly.

This people are, as it were, an advertisement that God takes out with the human race to show that he is present and at work in *every* human life, not just in the lives of Christians. By living the Christian life to its fullness, Christians are not the sources of redemption for others, but are rather living witnesses to others that God is at work in the midst of the Christian community, which is a *sign* of his faithfulness in working within *every* human community in some way.

Christian communities are "gift" to their world because people so easily despair when they are forced to rely solely on their own resources. They begin to think this is all there is, and doubt that there is more. When they see a community of men and women witnessing to the presence of a God who is loving Father and at work in human life, they are arrested in their slide toward despair; they are buoyed up and regain hope. Thus they are better able to resume the task of searching out how that same God is at work in their own lives.

It is my experience that in such a view we can see the culmination of a Spirit-led movement away from the notion of the absolute necessity of Church in the salvation of the world. Centuries ago, good Catholics believed that anyone not a Catholic could not be saved. That was not true then, and it is not true now.

The question to be put to the Catholic community at this stage of its development is this: *Do we really believe that the Catholic Church is necessary for salvation?* Let us be careful how we answer. Traditionally, we Catholics have been so impressed with our role in God's plans that we have given offense to others and have presented to them a picture of God nothing short of slanderous. By reading the "signs of the times" correctly, we may be able to improve on the performance of our forbears in faith in that regard, and usher in a new age of vitality and life for authentic Christian faith.

A Postscript

I had arrived at this point in my spiritual journey by the early 70's. It was a long way from my grade school days and the

Bark of Salvation, but as the TV commercial says, I still had a long way to go. It was not until I faced up to the thrust of contemporary Scripture scholarship and the theology of story that I would be ready to attempt an account of *Christian faith as redemptive intimacy.*

CHAPTER TWO

Correctly Naming the Present Challenge

I had long known that whenever Catholic people had found their faith particularly meaningful and lived it with joy and enthusiasm, it had always been in response to a particular vision of Church *and* the Good News of the Gospel. Reflection on my experiences had convinced me that the vision which had emerged from Vatican II, far from being definitive, was but a part of a larger process of evolution and development. This was continuing at so accelerated a pace that only the new post-Vatican II vision of Church which is aborning could do it justice.

Yet in the early 70's. I remained personally reluctant to publicly make the move toward the emerging vision of Church because to do so seemed to me then to require doing violence to the traditional understanding of Scripture and more especially of the Gospels. Like so many of my fellow Catholics, I felt uneasy because I sensed that there might be a conflict between Scripture and the emerging post-Vatican II vision of Church. That simply would not do. So if my spiritual journey was to continue, it would be necessary to address the problem directly and to gain a better understanding of just precisely how Scripture is to be normative for Christian life.

My strong academic background in philosophy and theology as well as my pastoral work with young people and adults had prepared me well to cope with the various visions of Church, but in addressing the contemporary understanding of Scripture, I was not nearly so fortunate. But the virtual revolution in contemporary Catholic biblical scholarship in our day helped to offset whatever lack I may have felt in this regard. Much, if not most, of what we Catholics had been taught about Scripture prior to 1960 was effectively neutralized or nullified by the appearance in 1964 of the Pontifical Biblical Commission's report, *On the Historicity of The Gospels,* and in 1968 of *The Jerome Biblical*

Commentary, which signaled for the masses the beginning of the contemporary era in the Catholic understanding of Scripture. I was much encouraged by this realization, because it meant that apart from the professionals, most of the rest of us were but beginners in the proper understanding of Scripture.

It is important to recall some recent history in the area of Catholic Scripture scholarship. To protect the historicity of Scripture at all costs, the Catholic Church for the first 43 years of this century effectively muzzled Catholic Scripture scholars. And in the 37 years since the appearance of Pius XII's *Divino Afflante Spiritu,* an encyclical on biblical studies which removed the muzzle in 1943, the fruits of that scholarship have been dammed up, as it were. This caused a reservoir of ever-increasing pressure that will inevitably break through the barriers and come cascading down full force on an unsuspecting Catholic community. If nothing is done to prepare more Catholics for what is surely coming in our understanding of Scripture, then the inundation will prove tragically traumatic for the faith lives of many. We could very well be on the verge of a real pastoral crisis, brought on by the stonewalling tactic of keeping from people for so long a time the known truth about Scripture.

Imagine the shock for the average Catholic in discovering: 1) that Matthew, Mark, Luke, and John did *not* themselves write the Gospels; 2) that the Gospels are by no means a biography or literal account of the life of Jesus of Nazareth; 3) that the Pontifical Biblical Commission in 1964 finally adopted the teaching of a goodly number of excellent Protestant Scripture scholars who had been teaching since 1919 that the Gospels do not so much reflect the times and life of Jesus of Nazareth as the life and times of the early Church between the years 70 and 100 A.D.; 4) and that some of the most important of the Pauline epistles were *not* written by Paul. And yet these are by no means substantive issues affecting anything essential in Christian teaching. When the results of the new Scripture scholarship go on to touch the central issues of our faith, the pastoral effect on the faithful could be nothing short of cataclysmic.

Put in concrete terms, most of the priests and most of the Catholic people in most of the parishes have been operating and are still operating with a view of Scripture that has now definitively been shown to be incorrect. This does not mean that Christian faith is suddenly invalidated, but it will require a change of theology and outlook. As more and more of the findings of the scholars trickle down into the Catholic communities, new impetus has been given to the formation of Bible study groups. While there has been a veritable Bible study group explosion in our times, this movement still involves only a minority of Catholics, mostly women, and the majority remains ignorant of and/or indifferent to the recent developments in this important area of Christian life.

Of course, the Bible study groups, like the communities from which they have sprung, are of two main sorts: those made up of persons who take offense at the slightest hint that things are not with Scripture as they were originally taught, and those formed around priests and teachers who are willing to face directly the truth emerging about the Bible in our times. If our pastoral strategies remain tied to the wishes of those believers who "take offense," there is little hope for a revitalized incarnational faith, and the parishes will remain for the foreseeable future caught in the grips of biblical fundamentalism.

The Fundamentalist Resurgence

Christian fundamentalism is on the rise because for many it is only by returning to the religious attitudes and practices of the past that we can stem the rising tide of paganism spreading across the world. There was a time, not so very long ago, when Catholic parents could be reasonably sure that their children would carry on the faith of the family. That is by no means the situation parents face today. The defections of our young from the Catholic faith to other Christian denominations, to other religions, or to the prevailing paganism have reached such epidemic proportions that one can hardly blame those who counsel a return to the past. One has to wonder whether the faith will die with us. Can the Catholic Church survive this onslaught or are we believers a dying breed?

Blame for the present predicament is cast all over the place. Our materialistic and pleasure-seeking culture rightfully gets a goodly share of the blame as the prophets of doom among us foresee the demise of Western culture according to a scenario which reads a lot like the fall of the Roman Empire. To counteract the self-destruct direction we seem to be on, many have counselled that we turn or return to the more religious fundamentalism of the past. If only we would return to those tried and true religious postures of a bygone day, we would be all right. Or so the story goes.

On the other side, while not denying the serious threat of the new paganism, others blame as well the institutional Church for not better adapting the Christian message to the present situation, but more especially for failing to really practice what it preaches in its own dealings with people. No wonder the young are not attracted to the Church. (As to whether Western culture is fated to follow the path of Imperial Rome, they are in no position to say.) But everything in their experience compels them to speak out against religious fundamentalism as a solution to anything. Whatever the true causes of our present problems, fundamentalism not only cannot solve them, it can only make matters worse by inhibiting the Spirit-led movement toward the renewed Church of the future. A return to the past would doom us to live out our faith lives in hypocrisy, publicly professing one thing when our experiences clearly reveal to us another.

The fundamentalist group won't go forward; the post-Vatican II group won't go back. To the former, the challenge of our day is to have the courage and humility to return to fidelity to the Christian Story as we have inherited it from those who have gone before us in faith. To the latter, the challenge of our day is to have the courage and imagination to take a leap of faith into the future, and to retell the Christian Story in ways which give new life. So it is that the Catholic Church is, in general, polarized between two groups of believers, all people who are serious about walking with the Lord, but who have diametrically opposed strategies for coping with the present situation.

Since I am myself a post-Vatican II Catholic of the second group, I have undertaken this account of my own spiritual journey in faith in order to suggest an alternative to the return to the past that so many counsel. That is not a very popular position to take these days when fundamentalism is on the rise and many in high places in the Church are talking and acting as if Vatican II were a terrible mistake. I have been moved to write this book in the hope that it might help to show that the real mistakes lie elsewhere, i.e., either in simply returning to the past or in taking Vatican II as the final word in the development of the Catholic Church in our lifetime.

Still, it must be admitted that at a time when the very fabric of our common life seems to be coming apart, fundamentalist religion becomes increasingly attractive. It dissolves all ambiguity and offers a clear and comprehensive account of both the problem and the solution.

Beset as we are with the uncertainties of life—the painful struggle to grow and mature as we fashion our lives into something truly meaningful, the inevitability of failure, suffering, old age, and death—it is only natural for us to seek some source of certainty and strength. Many find what they seek in their work (the Creative Solution); others get their strength by transferring out to another human being as if unaware of that person's own weakness and limitation (the Heroic or Romantic Solution); some give themselves over to noble causes and ideologies as their way of finding strength (the Ideological Solution); but the greatest number still plug into a transcendent God, that great power source in the beyond (the Religious Solution). The main reason for the resurgence of fundamentalist religion among the world's people is that it remains to this day the most apparently satisfactory human-made solution to the ever-present problem of human finitude. It is easy to see why this is so.

While it is true that human beings derive tremendous strength for coping with life from their work, the day inevitably comes when work no longer can keep us distracted. Heroes and lovers are so important in humanizing our lives and so helpful to us in coping with life's challenges that I am reluctant to say anything negative in that regard. But the truth is that our heroes and lovers are themselves only human, and so must find a source of strength beyond themselves, just as we must. If we expect them to sustain us to the end, we are doomed to disappointment. And no matter how noble the cause, a moment must come when it does not sustain us as it once did. Given the ultimate inadequacy of these so-called ''solutions'' to human finitude, it is small wonder that fundamentalist religion remains the most often used source of strength for coping, and the transcendent God the most effective transference object even in this day of such widespread unbelieving.

But the religious solution is not without its own perils. As Ernest Becker points out in *The Denial of Death* (Free Press, 1971, p. 259):

> If men lean too much on God they don't accomplish what they have to in this world by their own powers. How does one lean on God and give over everything to him and still stand on his own feet as a passionate human being?

Simply put, there is a price to be paid for adopting the fundamentalist position, and that price is the denigration of the human, which the Lord came to enhance. Of course, many still think this is a small price to pay for the "benefits" which accrue to the religious solution.

Fundamentalist religion may take many different forms, but its main characteristic, as I see it, is that it always absolutizes something human-made and then goes on to justify that move by declaring that what has just been absolutized is so by divine will. The advantages of that are not small. We create a very solid foundation for our lives, because the God who has just been absolutized by us can never surprise us, since he is in a way a being of our own making. We know what we have put into him, so we know exactly what we can expect to get out of him. We planned it that way. Thus we invest our lives with conviction and certainty, not to say fanaticism, which are the hallmarks of all fundamentalisms.

Nor is this temptation of recent origin. Throughout the long history of the Judaeo-Christian tradition—from the insistence of Israel against Yahweh's wishes on having a King, a Temple, and sacrifices, right up to the declared infallibility of the pope at Vatican Council I—we see the constant pressure for human-made absolutes. But in the Christian tradition, by far the most sacred and revered of the human-made absolutes is the Bible, which fundamentalists tell us is the "Word of God." Yet throughout that same long history the constant voice of Yahweh, the Faithful One, can be heard sounding in the hearts and lives of his people, calling them to give up the comforts of fundamentalist religion and to embrace the much more demanding ideal of incarnational faith.

Perhaps the greatest irony in the whole saga is the fact that Catholics have until recently been reluctant to respond to the voice of Yahweh *in their lives* because they somehow felt that that voice sounded only in the Bible or in the official pronouncements of the Church. So it was in the mid-70's that I came to the conclusion that when we Catholics cling so tenaciously to our human-made absolutes that we fail to recognize the voice of the Lord God in our midst, it was high time to rethink the prevailing account of the Christian enterprise.

Scripture: A Pastoral Account

In that task of rethinking, it would seem that the "theology of story" can be of important assistance to the men and women of faith of the last quarter of the 20th century. One of the most exciting and fascinating developments in contemporary theology is what has come to be called the "theology of story." Because the "theology of story" itself arose out of the recent Scripture scholarship, I have found that it can be helpful pastorally in introducing people to the fruits of that scholarship in a way they can more readily understand and accept. It is ideally suited to the task of updating Catholics with regard to their understanding of Scripture, and it is no accident that it should have come upon the scene precisely at a time when that is one of our most crying needs.

Thanks to the developments in contemporary Scripture scholarship, we have lost our innocence, so to speak, and can now see clearly the importance of "story" for human life and for Christian faith. As Elizabeth McKuen of Georgetown University so clearly put it in *The Theology of Story* (an address to U.S. Bishops' Committee on the Laity, April 14, 1978):

> It has fallen to us to become conscious of our story-telling role. Aware of the storied and man-made nature of our lives, we are no longer innocent with respect to the fact of our capacity to make meaning, *nor with respect to our responsibility for telling stories of God which allow life.*

What is judged dangerous and pastorally detrimental to the faithful in all of this is that it seems to undermine the historicity of Scripture. The Bible seems to become merely one more human-made "story" of God. It is hard to think of anything that would be more "offensive to pious ears," as we used to say. The crucial question then becomes: In what way is the Bible the Word of God? And in what way is it something of human origin that can be turned into an absolute in the service of Christian fundamentalism?

According to the Christian faith, the Word of God is the most powerful force on the face of the earth. It is the Word of God that created the world; it is the Word of God that transforms it into the Kingdom; and it is the Word of God that illumines our minds, enkindles our hearts, and renews and strengthens our lives. Techniques, pastoral strategies and programs are no substitute for the Word of God which is *the* motivating force in Christian life. On that much, all Christians seem to agree.

But when it comes to identifying the "Word of God" or how we are to gain access to it, the arguing begins in earnest among us. The Christian fundamentalists contend that the Bible is, in itself, the Word of God, which means that Christianity is a book-religion just like Islam. For Moslems, the Koran was dictated by God to Muhammed and so every sentence, every word, indeed every letter is of divine origin, giving to the whole the quality of immutable divine truth. All the answers are "in the book," and what is not "in the book" is not of much importance. We all know Christians whose attitude toward the Bible runs along these same lines.

Encouraged and motivated by the new Scripture scholarship, other Christians maintain that the Scriptures are not in and of themselves divine revelation, and so Christianity ought not be interpreted as a book-religion. The Christian Bible is not the Koran; it is not of itself absolute. It is not an eternal message dictated by God to creatures with no historical precedents. Rather, it is the historically dated account and testimony of human beings in particular circumstances regarding the presence of the timeless God in their own lives and in the person of Jesus.

The Bible *is not* the Word of God, but it can *become* the Word of God for us. The Bible becomes the Word of God for those who submit to its testimony in faith and so to the God revealed in it. Or to put it otherwise, the book becomes revelation for us only when we relate it to the presence of that same timeless God in our own lives and time. So what we find in the Bible is not God, but "God," which is to say, the presence of God *as interpreted by humans* and put into a witnessing narrative account or story.

The historicity of the Bible derives not from the literal accuracy and stenographic perfection of its accounts, but from the actual presence of God in those people at that time. But as soon as human beings begin to articulate their lived experiences of the presence of God, what comes forth from their lips is never God, but always "God." Thanks to the developments in Scripture scholarship, we now know definitively that the Bible is no exception to this basic law of creaturehood.

Of course, it will immediately be objected that this reduces Scripture to a mere compilation of human stories. But to even make such an objection one must assume that we have some way of capturing the reality of God in a verbal account that is not a story of human fashioning. It is to treat the Bible as the Moslems treat the Koran, and with the same result. We absolutize a human creation, reduce the God of mystery to an object fully expressible in human terms, and reduce Christianity to a fundamentalist book-religion, thus diverting it from what it really is, namely, an incarnational faith.

What distinguishes the Bible from other accounts of God is not that they are merely human stories (and it is not), but rather that it is, first of all, a human story of God's presence to the people of Israel, and second, a human story of divinity incarnate preeminently in Jesus of Nazareth and in each one of us. This ongoing ineffable *presence of God* to humankind is the true absolute of Judaeo-Christianity, which is why they are both incarnational faiths. This absolute simultaneously grounds the Bible, our faith, and our own lived experiences of the presence of God, and creates from the dynamic interaction of those three things what we mean by "revelation" or the "Word of God."

What makes so many Christians look at this view of Scripture with suspicion is that it seems to imply that the Bible is no longer "true." In response, it should be said that, of course, the Bible is "true." It is just that its truth is not necessarily either literal or historical. The Book of Genesis is an excellent example of this. Only the most rabid of fundamentalists continues to hold that the creation story is a literal account of how God made the world and that Adam and Eve were real persons. Even in my youth, standard Catholic teaching was saying that it was a midrash or poetic account, more like a parable than an historical account. This does not mean that the creation story in Genesis is either false or worthless; it means that we shall only be able to see its truth if we understand the kind of document Genesis is.

To that end, perhaps the following "story" might help. The life of a shepherd is often a lonely one. He is out on the hillside at night with his flock. The night is long and he craves human contact. Across the valley on a neighboring hill another shepherd experiences the same need. Each can see the other's fire in the distance, so in a game popular with shepherds the one reaches out to the other. He stands facing the other's fire, cups his hands around his mouth, and begins to sing out across the valley: "Oh, what a scourge to man is woman. She makes his life miserable with her plots and schemes. Her tongue is constantly going and there is no peace with her around. Out here in the hills it is peaceful—because she is not here!" His song or *decima* floats across the valley, echoes against the hills and immediately gets the attention of the other shepherd.

The listening shepherd knows the game well and realizes that he must make a response, but the response is to be a *contra-decima,* a song that takes an opposing view to the one his compatriot has taken. He rises, cups his hands and sings his counter-song: "Oh no, how wrong you are. What would man's life be without woman? She is his alter-ego, another self who completes him where he is wanting. Thus she is the source of so much joy; her presence makes one's heart leap for joy; life without her would be unbearable." The contest is on. Each shepherd adds stanzas to his song, alternating with the other, but he may not repeat what he has sung in any preceding stanza. The loser, of course, is the one who runs out of things to say. Such games helped the shepherds to pass the time and added a very human dimension to their lonely vigils.

The Book of Genesis is Israel's *contra-decima* to the *decima* of their pagan neighbors. Their neighbors said that human beings were an unfortunate creation, lowly and impotent, and caught between two opposing forces: the Supreme Principle of Good and the opposing Supreme Principle of Evil. Each of these deities used and abused people, and so humanity was but a helpless pawn caught up in a battle of the gods. To this day, the words of Genesis ring across the valley of recorded history as the *contra-decima* to any who would exonerate humankind for the introduction of evil into the world, and to any who would hold that there is more than one Supreme Being: Hear, O Israel, the Lord Our God is one! And since God didn't originate evil, then we must have. That was Israel's experience, and they put that experience into the Genesis account to offset the self-serving, copout stories of their contemporaries.

What we Christians have difficulty understanding is that the Book of Genesis is not an attempt at an accurate description of events that actually happened, but is rather a profession of faith by the Hebrew people in story form. Imagination and poetic license are important elements in all the books of the Bible, but this does not mean that they are not true. To say that the Adam and Eve story is not an account of actual events that happened to real people does not make that story untrue. The truth of that story, and of every story in the Bible, comes from its ability to integrate, unify, and illumine present human experience as valid, not from the objective and historical accuracy of the account.

The writers of the Old Testament took a real historical event from their history, and instead of recounting it just as it happened, they embellished it and made it heroic so that the story would contain a dream and an ideal which they wanted to hand down to their children and their children's children. The stories of the Old Testament were written hundreds of years after the events they portray and so they are not concerned with giving us those events in their historical detail, but rather they are concerned with sharing with us the religious or spiritual meaning of those events. They are looking back all right, *but they are not writing history*. They are mounting a dream, raising an ideal for themselves and their children, as if to say, if our ancestors were great because they responded to the Lord God back there, we can do it too, in our day. In fact, we can do even greater things if only we remain faithful to Yahweh.

We do much the same thing with our American history. We tell our children that Washington, Jefferson, and Adams were really great and we paint very idealistic pictures of these men. That isn't exactly the way it was with them, and we know it, but we are not lying. We are not attempting to tell the story of our founding fathers in an historically accurate way; we want to tell the story in a way that will impress our children and enkindle in them the understanding of and the desire for freedom and equality.

That is exactly what the Old Testament writers did with their heroes. Abraham, Moses, David, and Solomon are painted in very idealistic terms in the Old Testament. That is not exactly the way it was with them, but to have given an historically accurate account of the lives of these men would not have served well the meaning Israel saw in their lives.

For example, we now know that in the Exodus from Egypt the Israelites did not cross the Red Sea. The facts are that they crossed a swampy area called the Sea of Reeds. They were travelling light, having left most of their possessions behind, so they were able to get across the swamp with little more than the normal difficulty. But the Egyptians who were pursuing them were in full armor, with horses and chariots and all the engines of war. They came charging down on the fleeing Israelites and got stuck in the mud! That is the sort of story historical accuracy yields and which one would have to tell *if one were writing history*. But it wouldn't sell—not even in Peoria!

It was the faith of Israel that it was the Lord God who had delivered them from the Egyptians, and so they told the story of the flight in a way that would make it unmistakably clear that it was by the *hand of God* that they were set free. Hence the account of the rolling back of the waters of the Red Sea. It was not meant to be a history lesson, but it was meant to impress on future generations how great and good the Lord God was to Israel. From that perspective, the writers of the Old Testament were eminently successful, for to this day at the Jewish Seder that story is told and retold so that Israel might never forget.

So it is that the Old Testament is a thin skeleton of historical truth, fleshed out with heroic stories, which are professions of faith geared to moving the hearts of the Jews who read them to search for the validation of those stories in their own experiences. The truth of the Old Testament is to be found in the remarkable fact that so much of what it contains as revelatory is still being revealed in human experience today.

As Christians, we may not care much one way or the other how the Old Testament is interpreted. As heirs to the New Testament, we sometimes feel that the Old Testament is expendable, and that whatever is said of it does not apply to the New Testament, which is a totally different sort of thing. Incredible as it may seem, the similarities between the Old and New Testaments are striking. The New Testament is by no means a history of Jesus of Nazareth. About all we know historically about Jesus is that he was born, was very wise, attracted many people, and was condemned to death and crucified. After that, we don't know too much historically, but then again the writers of the Gospels were not interested in giving historical details any more than the writers of the Old Testament were. What then were the Gospel writers up to?

To understand that, it is imperative that we have some understanding of the distinction between Jesus the Nazarene and Christ the risen Lord of history. One easy way to do that is to recall that St. Paul never laid eyes on Jesus of Nazareth; it was the "risen Lord" whom he encountered on the road to Damascus. Now while Jesus of Nazareth and the risen Lord are not two different people, they aren't quite exactly the same either. It was the faith of the early Christians that Jesus of Nazareth had become the risen Lord. Their faith was in the risen Lord, and they believed that Jesus, the carpenter from Nazareth, by his resurrection had become the risen Lord. Jesus, as risen Lord, was alive and lived in them and could speak to them. So the Gospels are not really a biographical account of the life of Jesus of Nazareth, but rather the profession of what the risen Lord was revealing to the Christian comunities years and decades after the time of Jesus of Nazareth.

As a general date, the Gospels of the New Testament were written between the years 70 and 100 A.D., and were written from the point of view of those early Christian communities. What was being revealed to those communities by the risen Lord, who lived in those people and was present to them, was written down. As a literary device it was put in the mouth of the Jesus of Nazareth of the years about 30-33 A.D. The Gospels are remembering that Jesus, and so they are a kind of flashback. And just as we saw with regard to the Old Testament, the Gospel writers were more concerned with professing their own faith in what the risen Lord was revealing to them than with giving an historically accurate account of the life of Jesus.

Thus it was that Christians became Christians by telling and retelling the story of Jesus, and the Jesus-story became the profession of faith of the post-resurrection Church. But that story was never meant to be a literal account of the life of Jesus the Nazarene; rather it was the story of the risen Lord of history, who dwelt with his people, but the story was fleshed out and grafted onto the thin skeleton of historical truth which they had about Jesus of Nazareth. Like the Old Testament writers before them, the writers of the Gospels were looking back, *but they were not writing history*. They too were mounting a dream for their children, the dream the risen Lord was revealing to them. That dream, which is the central theme of the New Testament Gospels, is the Reign of God, the Coming of the Kingdom.

The Gospels are really the first Christians' profession of faith in Jesus as the incarnation of that dream. We Christians who read them centuries later still find them meaningful and true because what we find there is what the risen Lord, who dwells also in us, continues to reveal to us in our day. And it is that coincidence of traditional story and present experience that makes the Bible the Word of God. For the Word of God is what results whenever the risen Lord, who dwells in his people, speaks.

The Theology of Story

Once I had come that far in my spiritual journey I was only one step away from feeling free enough to attempt a retelling of the Christian Story for our times. The year was 1978, and in that year I was exposed to two things that helped me over the final hurdle. The first was John Shea's truly remarkable book, *Stories of God,* which appeared that year, and the second was the talk of Elizabeth McKuen on *The Theology of Story,* already quoted above. Shea likened each of us to Scheherazade—we tell our stories in order to live. That may seem a bit overstated to many, but not to me because it is confirmed in my own experience. Shea states on pages 41 and 44 why it is so:

The fact is we cannot leave anything alone. Everything we encounter is quickly and compulsively interpreted. We do not long abide experience in a fragmented, chaotic form. Shaping experience into patterns that are meaningful is the unceasing activity of the symbol-making animal. When our experiences do not easily yield meaning, we will "wring" it out of them or "bestow" it upon them. What will not be tolerated are unappropriated happenings. We will own, at all costs, what we undergo. . . .The instinct to meaning will not be denied.

I take that to mean that "human stories" are the normal carriers of meaning. It is "human stories" that create meaningful worlds for us to inhabit, and in the end, like it or not, we must concede that Christianity, as one of the most powerful creators of meaning the world has ever known, is in the last analysis a "human story." So if the Christian enterprise is in trouble with us, or with our children, or with our contemporaries, it could very well be because we insist on telling of our God by means of inadequate human stories.

Elizabeth McKuen spoke eloquently to that very issue in *The Theology of Story,* already quoted earlier:

Each age, each culture and each tribe tells a story about itself in order to create the meaning within which it exists. Our various identities within the human family depend on the continuity of experience over time which story telling provides. In the telling of a story—we know who we are. Traditionally, stories of God have provided an unconditional horizon for our lives. . . .But the simplest spiritual fact of our times is that these mighty stories of the acts of God have begun to lose their ability to provide the horizon and context for human lives. Many people can no longer hear those stories with the innocence of children. There are too many unanswered questions.

She then went on to conclude:

The difficulty in all of this lies not with God who in the final analysis exceeds the power of human language and is at least a mystery beyond our language, beyond image; the difficulty lies not with God but with man. For it is man who tells the stories, it is man who then takes them to be literal renderings of reality, and it is man who finally is painfully disillusioned when new experiences arise that are not adequately accounted for in the stories that he tells. *It is man, therefore, to whom we must turn for new and more adequate stories of God.*

I remember sitting in the audience that day in April and of experiencing those words: "It is man, therefore, to whom we must turn for new and more adequate stories of God"—as some sort of call. It suddenly seemed to me that all I had thought in my own spiritual journey had merely been preparation for my accepting the challenge she laid down that day.

Suddenly it was all clear. The fundamentalists were wrong. They were misled into thinking that the only way for Christians to remain faithful to their Scriptural heritage was for them to take the Bible literally and to faithfully rehearse the contents of Scripture rote-like until the end of time. They had come to that conclusion because they had started at the wrong end of the process; they had started with the results. The result of the revelation process was the Bible, and since it was taken to be in and of itself the Word of God, it became normative for Christian life as it stood.

Thanks to the new advances in Scripture scholarship, it is possible to look more closely at the process from which the Bible issued. And when one looks at the process rather than the results, it becomes clear that the proper location for divine revelation is human experience, and the chosen vehicle for the articulation of that revelation is human storytelling. The Bible contains the human stories which the sacred writer chose to convey the divine revelation contained in the communally funded experiences of a people.

If one looks carefully at this process, it is clear that fidelity to our Scriptural heritage demands more than simply conserving the results, it also demands that Christians of every age get into the process itself. But to do that each age must have its own *scribes*. We must do what the early Christians did, that is, we too must write down our accounts of the works of God in our midst. Scripture, far from preventing contemporary Christians from telling the Christian Story in terms of their own experiences, requires them to do so. This is all the more true for our generation because the once vital stories of God no longer give life, no longer give hope to contemporary men and women because they do not speak to *their* experience.

So it was that I came to the point in my spiritual journey where I felt not only free to tell the Christian Story from the perspective of my own experiences, but empowered to do so. The result is the account of Christianity that follows, which I have called *redemptive intimacy*.

CHAPTER THREE

Faith vs. Religion

In my experience, most Christians are people of good will not disposed to be obstructionist in the realm of the spiritual. What pains me is that so many good and loving people have been misled and so are laboring under one of the most debilitating misunderstandings the world has ever seen. It is a misunderstanding about something so essential to the Christian life that one wonders why more isn't being done to correct it. I am speaking of the almost universal opinion among Christians/Catholics that Christianity is one of the world's great religions. There is nothing in my life about which I am so absolutely certain as I am about the fact that Jews and Christians have been called to ''faith,'' *not* ''religion.'' If we fail to understand that, we cannot help but misunderstand the very heart of the Christian message.

The reason I am so adamant about this stems from the fact that for all of my adult life my experience has been quite consistent and clear on the matter. I cannot believe that those experiences have been in any way unique or special, so I cannot accept either that I am the only one having them, or that I somehow know something which is not equally and readily available to others. I, therefore, find it difficult to accept that anyone who has lived long enough to reach mid-life can have any excuse for not knowing that Christianity/Catholicism is a ''faith'' not a ''religion.'' Still, as we have already seen, religion remains a most attractive coping mechanism to many.

Religion: The Constant Temptation

This misunderstanding is not of recent origin, quite the contrary, from the very beginning fear-driven *religion* has always co-existed with the call to intimacy with God which we call *faith,* diluting and adulterating that faith, sometimes only slightly and at other times to a very high unacceptable degree. One basic reason for this is that the history of religion is a lot longer than the history of faith. When the call to "faith" was issued by Yahweh, religion had already existed among us for centuries. Faith was seen as a novelty, and religion is so deeply rooted in our nature and in our traditions that unless we are very careful, we almost inadvertently relate to God religiously, even when we think we are answering the call to faith. Another reason for the almost constant mixing of faith and religion is because religion apparently better serves human interests, needs and desires. We have a natural tendency to not let go of the religious elements in our lives, even when we are striving to be people of faith.

Ancient Israel encountered that very problem when it came into contact with the "religions" of its pagan neighbors. It was always the ideal of Yahweh that the faith of Israel *not* be mixed with the religiosity of their neighbors, but Israel succumbed again and again to the temptation to do just that. Despite the warnings of Yahweh and his prophets, the faith of Israel became mixed with the religious elements picked up from other cultures. So true is this that the Old Testament itself is a strange amalgam of faith and religion. To this day, the trick is always to know what in it is which. We Catholics are facing that same dilemma in the post-Vatican II Church, for much of what today passes for renewal is actually, on closer inspection, a reassertion of religiosity, not faith.

It is therefore unthinkable, to me, that anyone would attempt to tell the Christian story in "religious" categories. We really don't need one more "religious" version of Christianity. Not one. Such stories have proven to be ineffective in the task of capturing the minds and hearts of the young, and so at this moment in our history what is so desperately needed is for the Christian story to be presented from the perspective of "faith." Those of us raised on a "religious" version of our story, may be uneasy and find it difficult to make the shift, because to make the move from religion to faith requires one to make a radical change in the way she views herself, her world, and most especially her God.

In my own reflections on the matter, I have identified seven characteristics, any one of which is an infallible sign of the presence of *religion*. No doubt one or two of them may exist in persons of real faith, but when they all co-exist in the same person as they do in so many of us in mid-life, it does not bode well for the future of faith. Those infallible signs are:

1. Relating to God out of fear
2. Feeling the need to appease an angry God
3. Relating to God out of self-interest, i.e. attempting to get him to do *our* will
4. Viewing ourselves as little and unworthy in God's sight
5. Holding that there are two worlds, one in which we live, and another in which God dwells
6. Holding that some things in the world, e.g. sex, pleasure, etc. are in themselves evil
7. Violating the freedom and personhood of another by doing physical or psychological harm to her "in the name of the Lord."

Each of these items contradicts an element essential to being a person of faith.

If those are its telltale signs, then obviously religion is a very natural and normal response to human life. On the other hand, it takes personal effort to overcome this natural tendency and to consciously embrace incarnational faith. We create religions for the same reason we fashion anything else, to meet a human need. We produce religions and religion substitutes to enable ourselves better to cope with the uncertainties of life. It is fear which is the origin of *religion,* and that is what it essentially remains whenever it occurs in human life, i.e., a response to human fear.

Faith is an altogether different sort of thing. No response to human fear, it is rather the *ideal* presented to us by the Lord when he called Abraham out of his own land and made him our "Father in Faith." It is the ideal of the intimacy of God and all of humankind as incarnated in the Lord Jesus. Faith is the joining of God and man and woman in intimate communion. By faith we put aside our fears and self-interest and commit ourselves to God's dream for the world, i.e., that one day it will *be* the Kingdom.

By faith we come to see that there are not two worlds, one inhabited by humans (earth) and another inhabited by God (heaven), since by faith we know that God is intimately present to our world and to each of us. So long as we relate to God merely as a way of coping with the vicissitudes of human life, we have not yet reached the realm of faith. Faith is not a relationship to God made by humans for human purposes, but rather the literally unbelievable relationship which the Lord God himself initiated with our race for a divine purpose.

On reflection, we may be surprised and a bit disturbed by just how much ''religion'' still exists in each of us, and by how much religiosity remains embedded in Catholic practice. It is this religiosity, I contend, which keeps us from being truly free in the Lord, and which so offends our young that it drives them away from the Church. If we would once again attract and excite them, we must return to the ''faith,'' not to the religiosity of our fathers. That faith remains, when not diluted by religion, the most powerful force on earth for transformation, for liberty and for love.

Clearly then, the watch word of *religion* is: ''Fear not, trust in God and he will see to it that none of the things you are afraid of will happen to you.'' While the watch word of *faith* is: ''Fear not, the things you are afraid of are most likely going to happen to you, but they are not really the sorts of things that believers ought to be afraid of, and have very little significance compared to transforming the world into the Kingdom.''

On that basis, most of our world is religious in one way or another. Left to ourselves, we Christians, like our world, would invariably relate to God religiously. Of course, we have not been left to ourselves. According to Christian belief, God has personally intervened in human affairs, finally choosing to join the human race by incarnating himself in that man, Jesus. God, by incarnating himself in Jesus, also incarnated himself in *our* history, and in *our* very flesh. God dwells not in images, laws or rituals, not in Jerusalem, Mecca, or even Rome, but in people, in our noblest parts where justice and charity dwell. Throughout our history, his voice could always be heard sounding in the lives and experiences of his people, calling them to shun religion and to become a people of faith.

But the response of humankind to faith has been incredibly slow. Because of our addiction to religion and our fear of faith, we have altered the revelation, refusing to accept the God who is actually revealing himself to us, preferring in his stead a religious God of our own making. There are many religions in the world all of which believe in God. The uniqueness of Judaeo-Christianity, lies in the fact that (as a faith not a religion) it is based not on *our* belief in God but rather on *God's incredible belief in us*. He gave flesh to that belief by becoming one of us. He meant that act to be definitive, forever putting an end to humankind's demeaning love affair with religion. The great scandal and irony is that so many who call themselves Christians still fail to understand, and continue to commit themselves to ''religion'' in the Lord's name. Evidently, they have not understood that the dream of the Lord is frustrated as much by pious religiosity as it is by sin and evil.

A Relationship of Fear

Though fear is no stranger to us, it is not our constant companion either. Generally, we go from day to day untouched by fear, and there is an unspoken agreement among us that this is as it should be, for to be constantly fearful is to be neurotic. Common sense tells us that fear has no permanent place in a well integrated human life, and contemporary psychology confirms us in this attitude with everything from transactional analysis to assertiveness training. The message of common sense and psychology is clearly: don't let fear keep you from really living.

Primitive peoples may have lacked sophistication, but they were long on common sense, so they too knew the law of human nature that we simply cannot get on with living if we are constantly afraid. Some technique or strategy had to be found to cope with the fears which arose in them as they faced the awesome wonders of nature without any real knowledge of how nature worked. They hit upon a really effective way of doing that. They imagined that behind every natural wonder they didn't understand there was a controlling god or goddess who was intelligent, who had his or her own purposes, desires and interests, and who could, therefore be dealt with rationally.

Religion was thus born as a defense mechanism against the fates and as a way for lowly humans to work *their* wills in the world by negotiating with the superior powers which controlled it. It was a sort of bribe from the powerless to the powerful in order to secure for the powerless a life which could be rationally free from fear. That was a truly ingenious move, because it allowed life to go on. One ought not, perhaps, call it ''primitive'' because it still remains the prevailing strategy among us human beings for dealing with God.

When Judaeo-Christinaity is viewed as but a natural development of this religious attitude, it thrives on fear; it makes much of devils, hell and damnation, and it attempts to win hearts by scaring people half to death. Salvation becomes the primary and fundamental category, much as it is in the Bark of Salvation view of the Church.

Now what is so contradictory in all of that is the fact that in order to sustain that posture of fear of the divine, two assumptions have to be made, each of which contradicts the relevation that Jesus is. The first assumption is that God is somehow apart from humankind as our ''over-against.'' In order to be an object of fear for the human race, God must somehow be alien and apart from us. Yet the constant relevation of both Old and New Testaments is that God is not ''over against'' us, but has identified himself with us and is always *with* us. The second assumption is that this ''over-against'' is capable of doing us harm, of punishing us for all eternity if we don't do as he tells us to. Christians never have been able to make that fully compatible with the relevation of Jesus that God is Our Father, from whom we have absolutely nothing to fear.

Whenever we find ourselves cowering in the presence of God, it is a sure sign that we have lost our consciousness of faith and have returned to the reflex action of religion. Down through the ages the constant voice of Yahweh sounds: Be not afraid, I am with you! A pox on the houses of those who preach to frighten people into virtuous lives; a pox on the houses of those who reduce the Christian message to religious dimensions and burden and demean a people with fear. A fear-filled people can never truly be Church, for they can never truly be *sign*. Fear makes us incapable of witnessing either the presence of God or the Kingdom that is acoming. Faith empowers us to do both.

Appeasing an Angry God

A consequence of relating to God out of fear is that we then tend to view him as an angry and powerful adversary who must be appeased, which is to say pacified. Now while appeasement and pacification can be done in ways demeaning neither God nor human, when fear is the motive, even reparation and restitution tend to be reduced to spiritual pandering. To say that God needs to be pacified suggests the image of a petulant and narcissistic child who gives us no peace until it gets its way. Whenever the Scriptures speak of God in those terms, know that it has reverted to a religious version of its story.

I would venture the opinion that if the energy which the Christian people inordinately lavish on the appeasement of God were turned rather to the task of mounting the dream and witnessing the Kingdom, we would not now be asking ourselves why the Christian enterprise has so little credibility with our young. The fact is, the religious version of Christianity is itself incredible, that is it is not to be believed.

It simply will not do for us to paint a picture of God that violates the revelation which Jesus is. Jesus is the full embodiment of the graciousness of God. He is God's gift of himself to the world. Jesus is gift with a capital "G," and as such he gives all of humankind reason to hope.

Now Jesus couldn't embody the absolute graciousness of our God toward humankind if he were to give it only a conditional expression. If the Incarnation means that we shall be graced by God only on the condition that we do this or that, then with the Herod of *Jesus Christ Superstar,* we would be justified in saying to him: "You're not the Lord, you're nothing but a fraud!" To be the Lord is both to *be* and to *announce* to the world that unconditional gratuity of God toward humanity.

If that is the context of Christ's coming, then his founding of Church must be seen in that same light. Unfortunately, the Catholic Church has in many of its practices forgotten to give witness to divine graciousness. All too often it dispenses the spiritual goods which have been gifts to her with anything but graciousness. Conditions are set on almost every good the institutional Church dispenses, some of them harsh and unfeeling. Often we must appease, it seems, not only God but the pastor or minister as well.

The truth is that for people of faith appeasement never enters the picture. Human life teaches us an important lesson, if only we allow ourselves to learn it. That lesson is that the most precious things in human life like love, friendship, freedom, etc., are all gratuities which cannot be earned or deserved by our best efforts because they are "gifts." That is also the lesson of the Christian faith. In faith, we proclaim the unutterably wonderful fact that there are no obligations for the faithful since the whole Christian enterprise is from start to finish a gratuity. It is the gratuity whereby God has gifted us with his love and himself, and the gratuity whereby we give ourselves in love to him in return. The only proper response to a "gift" is a "gift."

Christ did not come so that God could begin to give himself to us, nor in order to make clear the conditions for salvation and forgiveness. All those things were given to humankind from the start without conditions. We have never been without them. To possess them, we need only accept the gift with pure hearts. *That* is the Good News of Christianity and Christ came to give all of humankind hope by making the literally unbelievable extent of divine generosity more visible. Since Church is the continuation of Christ's presence among us, it is only logical to conclude that this is her main mission as well.

A Self-Seeking Relationship

What is it that "turns us on" the most? As human beings, what is it that gives us all the most pleasure and satisfaction? That is a profound metaphysical question, because the answer indicates a major problem we all have in being human. Some may say that there is no one thing which pleases all. Some are pleased by money, some by power, some by fame, some by sex, some by learning, some by artistic creativity and by countless other things. But my experience has revealed that there is one single thing which we all seek amid those differences. What gives human beings the most pleasure, and in this we are not unlike God, *is having our own way.*

I am sure we can all relate to the following story which illustrates that truth. A wife at home gets a call from her husband at the office. "Honey, how would you like to go out for dinner this evening? Maybe we could get mother to take the kids, and after dinner . . . well, you know. How about it? Are you game?" Naturally the wife agrees, and as the final hours of the workday pass, expectation grows in both of them. She makes the arrangements with mother, and gets dressed up for her welcome but unexpected "date." He tries to keep his mind on his work, but finds it difficult as he plans the special evening and anticipates the love-making with which it will end. She hears the car pull into the driveway, and is radiant as her "lover" enters. The mood is irrevocably shattered as he takes one look at her and says: "Why the hell did you wear *that* dress? I wanted you to wear your sexy green one." Expectations dashed on both sides, angry words follow. They settle for TV dinners and spend the evening in sullen silence, hoping that it will turn out better the next time.

The point is clear. It is not sex alone which gives pleasure, but having sex the *way* we want it. So it is with all the other things mentioned which give us pleasure. We not only want them, we want them *our* way. What makes that human trait something of a tragic flaw is this: as finite human beings we cannot ultimately have our own way. We fail, we grow old, we get sick, and eventually we must die, none of which is the way we want it. So the human condition is such that that which turns us on the most is, in the end, unattainable by us.

Frustrated, we naturally turn to religion to ease the burden. We light vigil lights, we make novenas, we do extraordinary acts in the hope of getting God to give us what we want, to let us have our lives our own way. Eventually we may get so accustomed to dealing with God that way, that we stop relating to him in any other. We then work hard at mastering all the ways of getting God to be subject to our wills. That's religion with a vengeance, it is totally self-serving, and all "gift" has gone out of our relationship with God because we're constantly on the "take."

Faith changes that completely. Instead of thinking that the task is for each of us to be "good" so that God will give us what we want, the person of faith understands that Yahweh's primary call is not that we keep the commandments and stay out of trouble so as to be deserving of a reward, but that we become the living *signs* of his presence in the world and of the Kingdom that presence effects. Not breaking the commandments may well insure that we shall be called "good," but it is not nearly enough to make us a Sign-People, witnesses of a gracious and loving God. For that, more is required and it is to that "more" that faith calls us.

Unworthy in God's Sight

Religion makes us feel small and little in the presence of God; that is its essence. When we are constantly worrying about clearly marking the line which separates the infinite and powerful God who is Creator from the finite and impotent human being who is merely creature, we can be sure we are in a religious posture. Such grovelling was the hallmark of religion long before the call to faith was issued, and it has continued to be a litmus test for the diluting presence of "religion" within the Judaeo-Christian faith. I find it hard to understand how anyone who has really looked at the relevation can continue to take such things seriously. If we really are as mean and little as we are so often depicted by many in the Church, how are we to account for the fact that there is not the slightest shred of evidence that Yahweh ever looked at humankind that way in the Old Testament? And in the New Testament, we even have the account of the Lord God becoming one of *us*. There definitely should have been an eleventh commandment: Thou shalt not grovel!

In this regard, I never tire of citing the case of Ezechiel. According to the religious superstitions of the day, to see the face of God meant instant death. So it was that whenever the Lord Yahweh appeared to Ezechiel, who was no fool, he would hit the dirt and bury his face in folded arms. You can imagine how difficult that must have been for Yahweh, if every time he wanted to talk to Ezechiel, all he ever saw was his backside. (All God ever sees of religious people is their rears.) And so in a move which as well as anything marks the clear distinction between faith and religion, Yahweh Elohim in exasperation finally said to Ezechiel: "Son of Man, will you stand up so that I the Lord God may speak to you!" (See Ez. 2:1)

That should have marked the end for all time of religious grovelling but it hasn't. We feel uneasy in God's presence, we don't know what to do, what to say, so we hit the dirt and hide our faces from his sight. And yet Yahweh's message is: Stand up—it is I, the Lord God, who wants to speak to you. Don't you know who I am? Don't you know that I believe in you even when you don't believe in yourself? Stand up, I say. I am your Father. I have loved you from all eternity—be not afraid. Please. Look me in the face, for you are exceedingly precious in my sight.''

We can see the vestiges of the religious grovel in one of the potentially offensive versions of the final blessing. How often have you felt shrunk when a priest issues the command: ''Bow down your heads and pray for God's blessing . . .'' ? How much better it would be for him to have said: ''People of God, you are precious in his sight, stand tall now and receive the blessing of your God who calls you to be his own—in the name of the Father, and of the Son, and of the Holy Spirit.''

Religion deceives because it insists on placing emphasis on a single truth: the infinite chasm which, it contends, divides God from his creatures. Consequently, religion makes it harder for us to believe that God really loves us, that he forgives us, that he wants us to be truly free in his presence so we can be living signs of that presence to our world.

Because religion makes us lose confidence in that truth, we lose our handhold on it, and remain timid and unsure of ourselves thereby muting our witness of the Lord to others. We seem to live in the presence of God as tenants who after years of living in the same building with their landlord adopt an apologetic demeanor whenever he is present, as if their just being in the building were something of an offense. We give no evidence of feeling ''at home'' in our Father's house. Nor shall we ever feel ''at home'' there until we cast off our petty fears, stop grovelling, and in faith get a firm grasp on the relevation that we are the very sons and daughters of the Lord God. We therefore have not only the right but the obligation to have tremendous faith in ourselves just as we know by faith God himself does.

The Two-Worlds Theory

The origins of religion are firmly rooted in the two-world theory. As we noted above, primitive peoples found it helpful in coping with their fears to posit a second world, an invisible one inhabited by the gods who controlled the visible everyday world in which we live. The human race had always been very comfortable with the two-world theory, until, with the rise of science, the one-world theory of secularism emerged. One effect of that emergence has been to confirm many Christians all the more strongly in the two-world theory, and to give the impression that Christianity requires them to adopt that view.

It is that religious two-world theory which made it impossible for so many Christians in the past to understand the central theme of the New Testament, i.e., the Coming of the Kingdom. To religious Christians "the Kingdom" is that other world behind this one; it is the place where God dwells, the place to which we hopefully shall go when we die, God willing. This is a classic case of our natural disposition toward religion preventing our understanding of something essential to incarnational faith.

The Kingdom, first of all, is not a place. It is a state of affairs; it is the situation which obtains when God reigns and the Spirit rules. Secondly, the Kingdom is not to be found somewhere outside this world. It, and the Spirit-God who brings it forth, is to be found here. That is the relevation of faith, but we seem unwilling to accept it. Throughout the Bible, time and time again, the revelation emerges that Yahweh is God-with-us, that Jesus is Emmanuel, and that the task before us is transforming this world into the Kingdom, that is into a world in which God reigns and the Spirit rules. That is the ever present dream of Jews and Christians throughout the ages, a world of justice, peace and love. Religion would have us work to get out of this world. Faith urges us to transform it into the Kingdom.

To say all that does not in the slightest deny that God is also transcendent. What it does deny is that Judaeo-Christian revelation is concerned about God in his transcendence. If we hold strictly to what is revealed, leaving philosophy and theology aside for a moment, the constant message that emerges both from human experience and from the Judaeo-Christian Scriptures is that *God is here!* This is his world, and we are his people. His dwelling place is not in some invisible world beyond, but in the hearts of the people. That is why we can say of faith that it is always *incarnational*.

The experience of contemporary men and women is generally not of a God intervening in human affairs from another world. Few, if any, of us have ever experienced God as the Supreme Being who *intervenes* in our lives. Our experience is rather of the quiet God of intimacy who *is* our very lives. We become aware of him as powerfully present when our minds are illuminated, our hearts kindled, our lives strengthened, renewed, and touched by the power of love. Until we rid ourselves of the religious theory of two-worlds, we shall keep looking for God in places where he is not. Only by faith can we find him where he is.

Creation as Evil

Religion in America is strongly identified with the Puritan ethic, which is the stereotype that speaks most loudly to us of the presence of religion. Sex, strong drink, dancing, card-playing, partying, leisure, and other such things have all been singled out by religious Americans as evils to be avoided. It is something of a mystery why so many fundamentalists who take the Bible literally take that position, since it is in direct contradiction to the Book of Genesis.

Nothing in the world can be evil since God made it all and he looked on what he had made and found it good, indeed, very good. (See Gen. 1:31.) As we have noted above, the source of evil lies in the human heart and in the actions which come forth from it. Things aren't the source of evil, *we are*. About that the Genesis account is quite clear. That things are in themselves evil is one of several religious fictions invented to lessen human responsibility for evil by scapegoating it onto something or someone else.

In the Catholic tradition even the great St. Augustine, who clearly and consistently taught that the source of evil was the human will, seems to have fallen prey to this religious fiction from time to time. So filled with guilt was he over his own sexual excesses as a youth, that he came to hold that sexual intercourse was in itself evil for humans, and that only the desire for children could redeem what would otherwise be totally immoral. That sort of "religious" thinking continues to play an important role in the official versions of the Catholic Church's position on birth control. That fact alone might indicate the wisdom of rethinking that whole problem once again, but this time from the perspective of "faith." We must keep in mind St. Paul's assertion to the Romans: "I know with certainty on the authority of the Lord Jesus that nothing is unclean in itself . . ." (Rom. 14:14).

Harming Others "in the Name of the Lord"

In times like ours, when the fabric of life seems to be coming unstrung, perhaps the most attractive dimension of religion is the order and discipline it promises it can bring to human life. Faced with chaos, no society or people can long endure. Human life simply cannot go on under such circumstances. History teaches us an important lesson in this regard. A people will, for reasons of self-preservation, always prefer to give up their liberties and to reach out to the traditional imposers of order: government, armed force, and religion. As we have seen, the present meteoric rise of religious fundamentalism is in direct response to the growing chaos in society and the perception that things are now pretty much out of control. The revolution in Iran in 1979 was a textbook example of how religion is called upon from time to time to impose order on a society gone mad.

In every age, and in every community, there always seem to be religious leaders available for such duty, eager and ready to live up to the expectations of their people in times of societal breakdown. In Catholic history, the Crusades, the Inquisition, and the burning of heretics are some of the grim reminders of what can happen when religion is allowed free reign unchecked by faith. Nor should we leave out of our consideration the totally unacceptable treatment of women by and in the Church throughout our history. It continues unabated in our own times. There never was, nor could there ever be justifications *in faith* for such things. The so-called justification which are offered for continuing the domination and alienation of women, to put it bluntly, are all religious fictions of human making. That should be warning enough for us to know that the mix of religion with Christian faith has reached dangerously high levels and that the only effective remedy lies in a revival of incarnational faith.

The proper strategy of that faith is preserved for all to see in Acts 5:33-39. Gamaliel, a man of faith and a teacher of the

law, gave the Sanhedrin wise counsel when it seemed determined
to kill the apostles. He said:

> Let them alone. If their purpose or activity is human in its origins,
> it will destroy itself. If on the other hand, it comes from God, you
> will not be able to destroy them without fighting God himself.

The Christian Churches have always applauded the wisdom of
Gamaliel, since it postponed the martyrdom of the first Christian
apostles, but they have less consistently followed his advice
themselves with the obvious consequence that they have indeed
ended up "fighting God." All too often they have ignored the
parable of the wheat and the weeds (Matt. 13:24-30) and felt
themselves obliged to punish or harrass those they have judged
evil or misguided. Of course, the motives for such actions are
always pure: to insure salvation, to safeguard orthodoxy, to
insure moral integrity, and to protect simple believers from
anything judged detrimental to their belief and obedience. But
the road to hell is paved with noble motives. We must learn and
act on the lesson of Gamaliel and *leave people alone!*
    Our call is not to "force" others, but to "gift" them.
Whatever we say the effect of God's work in our world is, that
work can never be accomplished by force. It is our religious zeal
and our impatience for the Kingdom that lead us to think we can
hasten the process along by forcing people to do God's will as we
see it. Religion makes us very untrusting. We don't trust our
fellow human beings, we don't trust our God who has revealed
that he is at work in all of us, and we ultimately don't trust
ourselves either. That makes us fearful, and our fear causes us to
revert to force. When we do that, we proclaim to all the world
that we don't really know God, that we aren't really in tune with
his way of working in the world, and that we have abandoned the
strategy of faith in order to embark on a religious strategy with
which *we* are more comfortable.
    By faith, we know that God dwells in all people and that
he is at work in each one of us, and in our world, in ways we have
no sure knowledge of. If that be true, we have no alternative but
to follow Gamaliel's faith-filled advice. Our task in faith is to
witness to and be a sign of *God's* gracious presence not to effect
the salvation of the world. That is God's task. It is only when we

adopt the religious perspective, i.e., God is somehow absent from the world and dwells elsewhere, that we lose sight of our vocation and see ourselves as the only instruments for good in the world and thus feel obliged to take up arms against our fellows in the name of the Lord.

Conclusion

I am not so naive as to think that only a posture of pure faith is to be judged acceptable. Even in the finest moments of our history, faith has been mixed with religion, but in those finest moments the religious elements were not in ascendancy and did not dominate. As I read it, Vatican II was potentially the beginning of one of our finer moments, but the sudden rise in religious fundamentalism in response to the chaotic conditions of society worldwide now threatens to abort the foetus of that dream before it has a chance to come to term. Soren Kierkegaard once remarked: "Spirit is often suppressed by an abortion, men having several self-serving devices for suppressing the embryo of their highest life." I judge the present unrest in the Catholic Church to be the work of the Lord resisting attempts to undo the call to faith which came forth from the Council by the power of his Spirit.

But, as expected, the Spirit does not force us. We are at liberty to seize the moment and make it one of great faith, or we may choose to let it pass as another religious interlude in the ongoing story of faith. It is not at all a question of whether faith or religion will ultimately prevail, the triumph of faith is insured by the risen Lord dwelling in his people. The question is rather one of whether our age will respond to the Lord in *faith* or *religion*. That issue is still in doubt. Because it is, I have deemed it important to attempt to retell the Christian Story in faith categories. Having made clear what we mean by religion, we may now turn to what we mean by faith, beginning by getting back to our Jewish roots.

CHAPTER FOUR

Back to the
Jewish Roots of Faith

If ever there was a people who appear to have been engaged in religious fundamentalism, it was the ancient Hebrews. A reading of the first five books of the Old Testament, called the Pentateuch by Christians and the Law or *Torah* by the Jews, seems to allow of no other conclusion. Thus, the stereotype of the Jew as primarily concerned with minute laws, regulations and dietary purity has arisen, not without some justification, among Christians. That same sort of legalistic fundamentalism survives in our own day in many orthodox Jews. And yet . . . Abraham is called our "father in faith," and Pius XII reminded us that "spiritually we are all Semites." In our own time, Vatican II in *Constitution on Divine Revelation* (14) left no doubt on that score whatsoever:

> First God entered into a covenant with Abraham and, through Moses with the people of Israel. *To this people* which He had acquired for Himself, *He so manifested Himself* through words and deeds *as the one true and living God that Israel came to know by experience the ways of God with men,* and with God Himself speaking to them through the mouth of the prophets. Israel daily gained a deeper and clearer understanding of His ways and made them more widely known among the nations.

So whatever else may be said of the Old Testament, and regardless of how fundamentalistically religious it is in many of its elements, it also contains the beginnings of *faith*.

This should not surprise us, for though we may look on the ancient Hebrews as a primarily "religious" people, their pagan neighbors always found them particularly "irreligious." Who but the most irreligious would deny the existence of the gods, would insult them by not offering them honor and worship, and finally profane them by saying that the one true God dwelt not in some far off divine place but in the lowly people of Israel? Everyone knows that humans walk the earth, but that gods dwell in places most high and inaccessible to us from which they rule the world.

The Jews not only held that God dwelt *with them,* but they carried around the Ark of the Covenant and actually pitched his tent in their midst each night. No wonder they were always judged to be quite strange, if not mad, by their pagan neighbors. How ironic that centuries later the very descendants of those Jews, once themselves judged ''irreligious,'' would accuse the early Christians of exactly the same thing, and for exactly the same reason. In both cases, the accusers were quite correct in their assessment. It *is* ''irreligious'' to say that God is joined to humankind in such loving intimacy that he makes his abode with us because that was, and is, the very cornerstone of incarnational faith.

It is customary to mark the beginnings of that faith with the covenant which the Lord God made with the patriarch Abraham, a custom I intend to follow in the next chapter. But if that covenant with Abraham is central to Israel's self-understanding, then we would expect to find some pre-figuring of that self-understanding in the very first chapters of the Bible. And so we do. In what follows, I am indebted to Rabbi Joseph Soloveitchik who so brilliantly identified that prefiguration in his truly magnificent midrashic article: ''The Lonely Man of Faith'' in *Tradition* (VII, 2 (1965), pp. 5-67). What makes that all the more interesting is that it was Soloveitchik who led the Jewish Orthodox community in rejecting Vatican II's overtures for increased ecumenism between Catholics and Jews. He did so because he felt that they were two irreconcilable religious traditions. Evidently, he did not accept or did not want to discuss the fact that they have much in common as ''faiths.'' (Indeed, I would want to say they are the same ''faith'' though they are not the same ''religion.'') I find it particularly instructive that we should learn about the beginnings of ''faith'' from such a man. It only goes to confirm that religion and faith continue to co-exist in very strange mixtures.

The main theme of Soloveitchik's article is the existential predicament of loneliness, and how being a ''person of faith'' in contemporary society adds special dimensions to that problem. In the process of making that point, he naturally had to give his orthodox Jewish view of what it means to be a "person of faith." It is only with this latter point that I shall be concerned in this chapter. Soloveitchik turns his attention to the fact that the account of the creation of man given in the first chapter of Genesis is quite different from the one given in the second chapter. He wants no part of the accepted opinion among Scripture scholars as to why this is so, and prefers to suggest his own answer in his article (p. 10):

> We all know that the Bible offers two accounts of the creation of man. We are also aware of the theory suggested by Bible critics attributing these two accounts to two different traditions or sources. We reject this hypothesis. It is, of course, true that the two accounts of the creation of man differ considerably. This incongruity was not discovered by Bible critics. Our sages of old were aware of it. However, *the answer lies* not in an alleged dual tradition but in dual man, *not in an imaginary contradiction between two versions but in a real contradiction in the nature of man.*

So while Christians speak of two different ancient versions of the creation of human beings which somehow find their way into a single book, Genesis, Soloveitchik asks us to look on the two accounts not as disparate items which were later joined, but rather as two related and complementary accounts of the same thing. Or to put it more simply, we are not concerned with two stories of diverse origin, but rather with two parts of a single story, each part giving only half the truth. The whole truth about man emerges only if you take the accounts in the first and second chapters together as one story. He then proceeds to do just that, with amazingly revelatory results. In what follows, I have taken the liberty of putting those results into language more familiar to Christians, while in no way holding Rabbi Soloveitchik responsible for what follows, I do want to publicly acknowledge his inspiration since the substance of the thoughts is his.

Comparing the Creation Stories

By now almost all of us Christians agree that the Book of Genesis account of creation is not to be taken as literally true. It is a symbolic and poetic account charged with much more meaning and significance than any merely historical account ever could be. Theoretically, then, we are past worrying about the fact that there are discrepancies between the account of the creation of the human person given in Chapters 1 and 2 of Genesis.

In Chapter 1 we read (1:26-38):

God (Elohim) said:
"Let us make man in our own image, in the likeness of ourselves, and let them be masters of the fish of the sea, the birds of heaven, the cattle, all the wild beasts and all the reptiles that crawl upon the earth." God created man in the image of himself, in the image of God he created him, male and female he created them. God blessed them, saying to them, "Be fruitful, multiply, fill the earth and conquer it. Be masters of the fish of the sea, the birds of heaven, the cattle, all the wild beasts and all the reptiles that crawl upon the earth."

In Chapter 2 we read (2:7, 15, 18, 21-23):

The Lord God (Yahweh Elohim) fashioned man of dust from the ground. Then he breathed into his nostrils a breath of life, and thus man became a living being. The Lord God planted a garden in Eden and there put the man he had fashioned . . . to cultivate and take care of it. The Lord God said, "It is not good that the man should be alone." So the Lord God made the man fall into a deep sleep. And while he slept, he took one of his ribs and built it into a woman and brought her to man.

Now, as anyone can easily observe, there are four major discrepancies between these two accounts.

1. Adam and Eve I are made in the image of God and nothing is said about the origin of their bodies. Adam II is made from the dust of the ground and God breathed into his nostrils the breath of life.
2. Adam and Eve I are commanded to fill the earth and subdue it. Adam II is charged with the duty of tending and caring for the garden.
3. Adam and Eve I were created simultaneously and together. Adam II was created alone and only later was Eve II, created from his rib, given to Adam II by the Lord God.
4. In the creation account of Adam and Eve I, God is called simply God, *Elohim,* a general name for God used to talk about

the God of the Hebrews but also about the gods of other nations. In the creation account of Adam II, God is called the Lord God, *Yahweh Elohim,* a specific name for the God of our fathers, the Lord God of Israel who called Abraham out of his own land, sent Moses to deliver his people from bondage, and is the Father of Jesus.

Given the non-historical nature of the Scripture account of creation, it would be silly to ask which account is the correct one. That is not the point. The discrepancies are in themselves meaningful and instructive, for the two accounts are not at odds but importantly complement each other. Taken together they give the traditional Hebrew understanding of the human being. That understanding is part and parcel of our own tradition and it is on that base that all of Christian morality and spirituality rest. By reflecting on these four discrepancies we may gain new insight into the human condition, into the ambiguity we each experience in our own lives, and also into what it means to be a person of faith.

The discrepancies between the stories does not mean that Adam I and Adam II are two different people, but rather are identifiable parts of each and every human being. The creative, majestic, dominating Adam I co-exists with the humble, re-deemed, and God-fearing Adam II within every human heart. Since God created *both* Adams, and since each is simply striving to be what he was commanded to be by God, there is no sense in rejecting the one or the other. Rejection of either aspect of our humanity would amount to hypocritical and dangerous self-rejection and to our disapproving of a creation which God made and himself saw as "very good."

The Story of Adam I and Eve I

The essential traits of Adam and Eve I quickly come into view if we consider their story from the perspective of each of the four discrepancies which we have identified.

1. Adam and Eve I were made in the image of God. For Christians, this means that we are somehow made in the image of the triune God and that, like him, we are capable of knowledge and love. A Jewish interpretation of that fact of being made in God's image differs from ours. In the Jewish tradition, the fact that we are made in God's image is evidenced by our unsurpassing dignity with respect to the rest of nature. Like God, and unlike the brutes, we are creative, i.e. we are able to produce order in our world. Like God we can make laws, and so are, by his will, the "lords" of nature. We are not so much subject to nature as we are charged and responsible with controlling it. This is the strongest sign of our great dignity and of the fact that we are made in the image of God, the Creator.

A moments reflection indicates how true that is. *We* create the many worlds in which we live. Who but we humans created: the world of high fashion, the world of sports, the business world, the world of technology, the world of pornography, the world of religion, the world of high cuisine, the world of drugs and alcohol, the world of medicine, the world of academia, etc.? The list is endless. Granted that some of the worlds we have produced are really unfit for human habitation, the fact remains that our ability to create these worlds proves that we were made in God's image.

Ancient Israel's understanding of that truth is beautifully expressed in Psalm 8:5-10:

> What is man that you should be mindful of him, or the son of man that you should care for him? You have made him little less than the angels, and crowned him with glory and honor. You have given him rule over the works of your hands, *putting all things under his feet:* all sheep and oxen, yes, and the beasts of the field, the birds of the air, and the fishes of the sea, and whatever swims the paths of the seas. O Lord, our Lord, how glorious is your name over all the earth!

Humans do not merely co-exist with the rest of nature, they are blessed with reflective, creative, imaginative, and intelligent life, thus reclaiming themselves from such co-existence. Blessed with all these things, we are also blessed with all the resources necessary to achieve our God-given goal. But since this story of Adam and Eve I is a story of human dignity and power, no mention is even made of their bodies, which are signs of limitation, weakness and of their ultimate mortality. No, Adam I and Eve I are success oriented, regal, and suited, like the God in whose image they were made, to create worlds and to rule the worlds they have made.

2. Adam and Eve I are to fill and subdue the earth.

But it was the experience of Israel that there was no real dignity without responsibility, and no responsibility without living up to one's life commitments or vocation. Animals can simply exist because they are not responsible for anything. Not so with us. A second clear sign of human dignity is to be found in the fact that Adam and Eve I are charged and responsible for filling the earth and subduing it. But if that is their charge, then they must learn and understand how nature works.

By necessity of their vocation, Adam and Eve I are very pragmatically oriented; their minds turn almost automatically to the "how" questions. How does the cosmos function? How can we make it function to our own ends? Intellectually, they have a keen interest in all those kinds of knowledge which will allow them to gain control of their environment. They do not have much interest in those other intellectual functions, e.g., literature, poetry, imagination, fantasy, dreams, etc., because none of them contribute to helping them dominate their world. Adam and Eve I are aggressive, bold and success-oriented, but in being that way they are merely following the mandate of God that they subdue the earth. When they succeed in doing that, they are not rebelling against God, they are merely being themselves, being what he made them.

We all know people who fit perfectly the descriptions given of Adam I and Eve I. American culture seems to have been built on this single dimension of the human personality. But more than that, we are able to identify an Adam I or an Eve I at our own center. We strive to dominate, to control, to succeed, and we are quite correct when we say we cannot do otherwise because that is our essence. Of course, we must quickly add that it is not our *whole* essence. That message remains an integral and essential part of ancient Israel's *contra-decima* to the world. We get in trouble only when we take Adam and Eve I to be all that we are called to be, and ignore the other half of the story.

3. Adam and Eve I were created simultaneous and together. Adam I and Eve I were never alone, not even from the first moment of their creation. They were created simultaneously and together, and hence were always part of a larger social grouping. This was as it should be, for no individual could possibly subdue the earth alone. Challenged by an environment which they cannot subdue individually, they can only live up to their responsibility by "working together." So the group into which they were created is a perfectly natural one, it is a work group. Eve I was created along with Adam I; she is therefore equal to him as a work partner.

Though they work together, they do not "exist" together. Their surface personalities are joined in a common work of successful production, distribution and consumption of goods and in subduing the earth to their own interests. They need each other both to survive and in order to succeed. But their liason is forged by the indomitable desire to triumph; it is a purely utilitarian dual relationship consisting of an "I" (Adam I) and a "Thou" (Eve I) who collaborate solely to further their own self-interests. Adam I and Eve I were charged with subduing the earth, not with the task of creating true community, nor with sharing their in-depth personalities with one another thereby cleansing, hallowing, and redeeming their existence. They are much too busy for that. They are, after all, merely co-workers, not friends.

Undoubtedly, this strikes us as a rather one-sided and sterile account of man-woman relations. But we should remember that it is being presented as only one half of the picture and it was not intended to be the whole story. Yet for many of the young in America it is just that. Having eschewed parenthood, they seem locked into a totally self-serving relationship. The goal is simply to create their own world of pleasure and security, and to that end they jettison all those things which older and wiser cultures have found cleansed, ennobled and redeemed human existence. More than that, the self-serving relationship of Adam and Eve I is being held up as *the* model for people to follow. Clearly the truth of the Adam and Eve I story is being confirmed once again in our own times.

4.   God is a God of power and might. Adam I and Eve I were made in the image of a God who created and now rules the cosmos. He seems to be the God of nature, the God of the philosophers, the maker and ruler of the universe. Called to share in and image the great dignity of such a God, there seems to be little intimacy between Adam I, Eve I, and their God. It is almost as if their relationship with God, like their relationship with one another, is merely a pragmatic one. (One is tempted to say, in the light of the preceding chapter, a merely "religious" one.) There is nothing particularly redeeming about the way Adam I and Eve I relate to their God because there is no sign of weakness on either side. It is purely a collaboration of power and might for reasons of self-interest.

No wonder, then, that the word used to speak of such a God was the common name *Elohim,* for Israel knew that their God was a redeeming presence who had actually revealed his name to Moses. It would have been insulting to Yahweh to have used his name in the Adam and Eve I story. For Yahweh, by revealing himself to Israel, also revealed to Israel that human beings are not merely Adam I's or Eve I's, for deep within each of us there is also an Adam II or an Eve II. We must now turn to that part of the story, for it is there that ancient Israel recorded the first beginnings of faith.

The Story of Adam II and Eve II

1.   Adam II was fashioned of dust from the ground. He can never forget his humble origins. He never forgets that the breath of life in him is not of his own making but is of the Lord God. Adam II knows from his own experience that dignity, majesty, dominion and success are not the sole objects of human questing. Being made in the "image" of God is not enough for Adam II, it does not satisfy a hunger he feels deep within himself. He longs for an intimate, living relationship with a personal God. At his center, when experiencing his own selfhood, he is aware of another self—the Great Self. He realizes that a life of dignity and power may very well be an unredeemed life. He knows that redemptiveness is achieved not by the forward surges of Adam I but yielding to a higher and truer Being. Redemption is not born of power and might, but of shared weakness and failure, which are the lot of every person as finite.

Human experience seems to corroborate the experience of ancient Israel. We have all been in situations when someone or other comes on like Adam and Eve I. What is our reaction to those who come at us with power and might? They try to control the situation, they try to impress us with how much they know, how competent they are, how successful they have been and how many influential people they know. As their performance unfolds, we feel ourselves receding farther and farther away from them. We are repulsed. Psychologically we move *away* from them, as if to better protect our delicate psyches from their onslaughts. But if and when we meet someone who shares with us out of their weakness or troubles, we find ourselves moving *toward* them out of compassion. We are attracted. This experience, better than anything I can think of, shows why it is that Adam I and Eve I cannot live redeemed lives.

Of course it is not easy for us to be present to one another out of our weaknesses. Each of us has a desire to be well thought of by others. Often we play games, pretend, put on masks and engage in other strategies aimed at showing just how wonderful we are and how fortunate others are just to have us around. If we would lead redemptive lives, we must unlearn those automatic defense mechanisms and learn to share deeply with others even the dark sides of our personalities, and we must also learn to allow others to do the same with us.

2. Adam II had to tend and care for the garden. If Adam and Eve I are called upon to rule and to be regal in their bearing, then Adam II is called upon to serve and to minister. The image used to convey this call to service is that of a gardener who lovingly tends and cares for a garden. Adam II lovingly tends nature, however, because he is preoccupied with finding the Lord God there. He must find and get in contact with the very source of his life. He does not relate to nature, then, as Adam I would. He does not try to make nature work to his own ends. Rather he seeks union with his God, and views all of life as God-filled. He approaches his environment as mystery in song, poetry, imagination, and celebration. Adam II attempts to cultivate and develop those parts of his intellect and personality that get beyond the manipulative use of knowledge and psychic energy to rule and to dominate. His life-search is not for success and control, but rather for a reunion with the Lord God who breathed the breath of life into him in the first place. He will never feel whole and complete or be freed from his existential loneliness until he succeeds at that.

This interpretation of the vocation of Adam II underscores an often ignored truth: The human person was made to serve. Generally, under the impact of male chauvinism, we have interpreted that to mean that women are to serve à la Adam II, and males are to dominate à la Adam I. But Eve II has not yet arrived on the scene. The vocation to be servant was addressed to Adam II, and it is therefore unjustified to twist the truth of our nature in such a way that only women are seen as called to service. Of course, it is equally fallacious to turn the whole thing around and to say, as some feminists at times seem to, that the call to equality in the workplace and assertiveness is the only call. We cannot live in the truth of our nature unless we recognize that the call to success and the call to service are addressed equally to both men *and* women.

3. Adam II finds himself alone. That aloneness is intensified by his realization that he is absolutely unique and unlike the rest of creation. The Lord God recognized Adam II's problem, so Chapter 2 says he formed the animals and brought them to him so that he might name them. Burdened by his existential loneliness, Adam II takes the head of each animal lovingly in his hands and looks into its face before naming it. He is insecure because he cannot find in all of nature a reciprocal gaze. He is the silent watcher, never being watched. He alone in all of nature has no companion.

It is hard for us to imagine what it would be like to be in that predicament. We get some sense of that if we go to the zoo alone. We walk from cage to cage looking into the eyes of each of the animals in silence. There is no "human connection" between us and the animals. We cannot speak to them, but more importantly they cannot speak to us; indeed, they have nothing to say. To be the only human in such circumstances would be unbearable. Yet, so the story goes, that was the very situation in which Adam II found himself.

But human companionship is not to be achieved through conquest, nor by anything Adam II himself can do. It can only be achieved through surrender and it can only be accepted as "gift." Adam II would still be alone if he had not been overcome by sleep, for it was in the defeat of sleep (defeat in the Adam I sense, since when one sleeps he is no longer in control) that he was to find a companion, another self. But sleep and letting go were not enough to gain for Adam II his fondest desire. He had to sacrifice and surrender a very part of himself for Eve II.

Companionship and a redemptive community (unlike the work group of Adam I and Eve I) are sacrificial gestures. They require the gift of self for the other. The work group of Adam and Eve I was not enough for Adam II; he wants a new fellowship, an existential community in which not only hands but experiences and hearts are joined in a single rhythm. *He craves personal (not necessarily sexual) intimacy.*

But intimacy is a gift from the Lord God. For Eve II was introduced to Adam II by the Lord Yahweh. *And thus was born the first redemptive community,* which unlike the work group of Adam and Eve I involved three not two. There was an "I" (Adam II), a "Thou" (Eve II), and a "He" (Yahweh) in whom all being is rooted and finds redemption. In this account of the creation of Eve II, we have the seed of a faith and covenant-community that was to reach its high point for the Jews in the covenant relationship forged later between Abraham and the Lord Yahweh.

Christians, not recognizing the real meaning of this story of the first redemptive community, have too often put it to use for anything but a redemptive purpose. It has become a commonplace to point to the second chapter of Genesis to justify the cultural and ecclesial inequality of women. If woman is derived from man, if she is merely his rib, then obviously she cannot be his equal. The irony in that is that the story establishes just the opposite conclusion. Let me try to show how it does so.

Adam II cannot find in all of nature a reciprocal gaze—that is, he cannot find himself in nature. He is the silent watcher, never being watched. No one in nature looks back at him as another self. Lonely and isolated amid the grandeur and glory of creation, he experiences untold pain. Then one night he is awakened by the Lord God. "Adam! Adam! Wake up, Adam!" Adam awakens to the presence of the Lord God. "Yes, Lord, you called?" "I did, Adam. Adam, *look what I've got for you!"*

Adam turns and there she is. She is beautiful. She doesn't have a stitch on. He looks at her but is not aroused. He is staring intently at her eyes. He is seeking a reciprocal gaze. Their eyes meet, and he exclaims with joy, "My God, you're me!" Only another self, only an equal could reveal to Adam his very self and return a reciprocal gaze. Eve II is Adam II's other self and hence his equal. It is a cruel distortion to use this mythic story to ever justify making her anything less.

4. Adam and Eve II are not satisfied with being "images of God." They shared in his power to rule nature, but they long to enter into an intimate, personal convenantal relationship with their Lord God, who is the source of the very life in them. But it is not up to them to bring that about. If that were ever to happen, it would have to be initiated by the Lord God, himself. And so it was for Israel, for Yahweh Elohim, the Lord God of Israel entered a covenant with Abraham and revealed his very name to Moses. The deepest yearnings of Adam II and Eve II can only be satisfied, then, by Yahweh, the God of intimacy, the God of the togetherness of God and humankind, the God of our fathers, the God of faith and the covenant.

The Human Paradox

Adam and Eve I and Adam and Eve II never actually existed, as we have already seen. They are rather imaginative, literary creations which the sacred writers, under the inspiration of the Holy Spirit, chose to use to give their message of faith. But it has always been possible to discern in human life two contradictory motives or urges: 1) the urge to succeed, to dominate, to be special, and to stand out from the crowd; 2) and the urge to escape isolation, to avoid being thrust back on one's own energies alone, to merge with others in a redemptive communion of some sort. The first drive or urge is typified by Adam I, the second by Adam II.

To identify these powerful drives in human life is not to solve the problem of how to live with both of them together. For if I give in to the first drive too much, I run the risk of failing to come to grips with my natural dependency and I cut myself off from the healing power of communal love. If I give myself over to the second drive exclusively, I run the risk of failing to develop all of my potential and of making my own personal and special active contribution to life.

Ernest Becker, in his Pulitzer Prize-winning book, *The Denial of Death,* has called this predicament the *ontological paradox.* He claims that it can never be satisfactorily solved, and that the most we can ever hope for in this life is to cope with it more or less well at each stage of our development. We must constantly fine tune our lives, adding more redemptive intimacy when that seems appropriate, and adding a bit more ambition and self-fulfillment when we are on the verge of being submerged in or smothered by the community. Only the truly wise and virtuous among us know when to do which and to what degree.

If Becker is correct, and I am inclined to think he is, then it will not do to say that we must all become Adam II's and Eve II's. That sounds noble and uplifting, but is totally unrealistic. For as has been observed, God created *both* Adams and *both* Eves, and called each to be what they are. The challenge is always to find a way to live up to both parts of our vocation to be human.

Much of the confusion over the roles of men and women in our culture stems from a failure to understand that. It is generally accepted in our society that men would be predominantly Adam I's and that the women would be predominantly Eve II's. This overlooked the fact that deep within every male is a burning desire for redemptive intimacy and deep within every female there is a burning desire for achievement, success, status, and affirmation. The truth is that traditional role models are inadequate for both men *and* women.

Having recognized this, women have begun to search out ways of bringing the Eve I in each of them to the fore and men have begun to understand their hunger for redeeming lives and so search for the ways and means of giving the Adam II in them fuller expression. All of that is to the good. But what a tragedy if, in that process, women become exclusively Eve I's and men exclusively Adam II's! That would mean we would have the same problem as we do today—but only in reverse. Down through the ages, the *contra-decima* of the faith of Israel sounds in our ears. We are to move to neither pole exclusively, but are to strive to live firmly holding onto both dimensions of our God-given human personality. But as Ernest Becker has shown, that is much easier said than done.

Time I and Time II

As we might have expected, if the human vocation involves work and achievement alongside redemptive intimacy, then it should be possible to look at the days of our lives in that light. The time we invest in being Adam I or Eve I is qualitatively different from the time we invest in being Adam II or Eve II. It is unfortunate that in English we have only the one word "time," and that we have to use it in both cases thus giving the impression that they are the same.

The Greeks had two words for "time." *Chronos* was the word they used to designate time in general. For example, "Spring is the most beautiful time *(chronos)* of the year." But they also had another word, *kairos,* they used to designate the right time, the acceptable moment, the exact or opportune time. For example: "Now is the time *(kairos)* to invest your money in energy-related stocks."

Following that lead of the Greeks, the Christian tradition has distinguished two entirely different kinds of time. Time I *(chronos)* is linear time, secular time, the time in which I am moving and accomplishing and doing things. It is Adam I time. It is the time of which we say that it is "spent" or that it is "lost"; it is the sort of time that can be "used up" or "wasted." I never seem to have enough Time I; it moves too fast and seems always to be ebbing away. I have less Time I in my life today than I had yesterday.

But Christians also like to speak of another sort of "time"; we may call it Time II *(kairos)*. It is special time in the sense that it is the time in my life when special and sacred things happen. It is the time when I have special insights into reality, as if seeing things in a new light. It is the time of peak experiences, of altered consciousness. It is the time when I am most my truest self. It is the time when I have it all together and act not out of my needs and compulsions and not in order to accomplish something or get something done. It is the Adam II time in my life. Time II is the time of intimacy, when I am building relationships, when I am cultivating friendships that are not pragmatically self-serving, when I am loving, or when I am just alone with myself. We never speak of Time II as being ''spent'' or ''lost'' or ''wasted''; it is ''time saved,'' or better, it is the salvation time in my life.

Amid the hurly-burly of everyday life, and given our natural inclination to always be accomplishing something à la Adam I, it was only natural that when it came time to relate to God, we began doing it religiously, à la Time I. Later, when the call to faith sounded in the experience of Israel, it was clear that it was a call to redemptive intimacy with God and with one another, for which Time I was totally inadequate. If we were to lead redeemed lives, Time II was going to have to become much more important to us. We were going to have to become persons of faith, and change the way we looked at ourselves, our world and at God. Israel, though first to hear the call to faith, was incredibly slow to give up religion and embrace faith. Yet it did manage to keep the dream of faith alive and hand it on down through the ages until from the root of Jesse of the line of David sprang *the* Person of Faith—Jesus of Nazareth. It was from Jewish roots, then, that faith blossomed into the Christian Story.

CHAPTER FIVE

A Proclamation
of Christian Faith

Whenever I think of proclamations of faith, I cannot help but recall a sage remark by Carl Sandberg, "Nothing happens unless first a *dream*." And once I remember that remark, another immediately comes to mind. "It is my *dream* that makes me what I am." It used to be said that you could tell a man by the company he kept, but I think it is equally, if not more, true that the measure of each one of us is the *dream* we cherish at our center. What sort of hopes, ideals, and aspirations we have for ourselves and our world are of the utmost importance, because whatever they are, *they* make us the kind of people we are.

Jesus understood this very well, and that is why in his own ministry he was constantly offering people a new dream. If we want to change, or if we want others to change, we must begin either by getting a different dream at our own center or helping others to do the same. Doing that for others is an essential ingredient of every ministry which aspires to be "Christian."

For two years, 1976-78, I was a consultant to the Parish Renewal Institute of Chicago whose main objective was to help pastors in the work of renewing their parishes. Two networks of parishes were formed, in Toledo and Chicago, and one of the first steps was to have the participating parishes produce "vision" statements. To many, that seemed more acceptable than calling them "dream" statements, but in the end that is what they were. To help each parish produce its own concrete specific and individual "vision" statement from its own experiences, the Chicago Network produced a more general one as a trial model. I was on the committee that finally produced the network vision statements, which almost immediately fell into disuse because the parishes were so eager to fashion their own.

I have decided to reproduce the Chicago Network statements at this point because they still represent for me what we should be saying to one another ''in faith.'' In addition, by including them here, I hope I shall give them a broader circulation and also afford myself a long-awaited opportunity to comment on them. It should be kept in mind, however, that these statements were originally meant to be proclaimed orally in public, not to be read silently in private. (I suspect that remains the best way to first encounter them.)

Our Story

1. It all began when God called Abraham out of his own land. ''Look around you, Abraham, things are not as they should be. Everything is out of joint, it is not my dream, it does not speak my presence. Leave it all and start anew. And if you do, I shall be your God and you will be my people.'' According to the legend, Abraham believed and left the land of his fathers trusting in the promise of God.

Yet that trust was tested again and again, the severest test coming in the call to sacrifice his only son, Isaac. Scripture ends its account of that event with a renewed promise from God to bless Abraham and all his descendants. But an ancient oral tradition among the Hebrews carries the story on a bit further, revealing Israel's role as *sign*.

2. According to that oral tradition, everything is over and God is about to leave when Abraham says, ''Wait a minute. You may be through with me, but I'm not through with you.'' God said, ''All right, what's troubling you now?'' Abraham replied, ''If you are all-knowing, then you didn't need this proof of my faith!'' God answered, ''No, I didn't.'' Abraham continued, ''I may be a sinner, but a miserable sinner I am not. I know that I have been faithful to you, so I didn't need this proof of my faith either.'' And God said, ''No, you didn't need it either.'' Then Abraham became angry and asked, ''Then why the hell did you make me go through it?'' To which God replied, ''I didn't need this proof. You didn't need this proof. But the *world* needed this proof as a *sign* that there is such a God as I.''

3. Thanks to the fidelity of Abraham and his descendants, the dream and the promise were kept alive among wandering nomadic tribes until the time of Moses, the first of the great

prophets, when the dream became incarnated in a people, Israel. Moses, because he was a Hebrew raised as a prince in the house of the Pharaoh, had a deep sense of what real freedom and dignity were. One day he killed an Egyptian guard who was mistreating a Hebrew slave, and was himself forced to run off into the desert to save his life. It was while wandering in the desert with the nomadic tribes that he came to know the God of Abraham, Isaac and Jacob. God appeared to Moses and commissioned him to go back to Egypt to free his people from bondage. "Moses, I am the God of your father, Abraham. I want you to return to Egypt and command the Pharaoh to let my people go!" Moses said, "How shall they know that it is *you* who sent me? What shall I say to them?" God said, "Tell them that he who is with them, he who walks with them and is present in their midst as he promised their father, Abraham, it is he who sends you. For I am the-God-with-his-people, the God of freedom, I am Yahweh, the Faithful One."

So begins the most remarkable story in all of human history, the story of the Covenant, i.e. the story of God's loving presence to all of humankind and that special people he forms in every age to be the living *sign* of that redeeming presence. For with the Exodus was born that beautiful tradition of the Hebrew people, to which we also are heirs, that they were not only called to freedom themselves, but were called to be the very *sign* of God's liberating presence in the world.

4. But like us, the Hebrews were high on ideals and low on performance. Almost immediately they began to grumble about their hard lot in the desert. Bondage in Egypt was so safe and secure compared to walking with the God of freedom. That was risky business, indeed. The-God-with-his-people was so frightening a thought to them that they yearned to distance themselves from him, to locate him somewhere "out there." So one day, after Moses had been gone for weeks on Mount Sinai, they persuaded Aaron to hold a festival to honor the God who brought them out of Egypt, and to build a golden calf in his honor. The anger of God and of Moses at this sight was not because the people had turned to pagan idolatry, they were to do that only much later in their history, but because they had turned from faith back to religion. They had tried to rid themselves of the sense of

God's presence among them. Instead of seeking him in their relations with one another, they had tried to "locate" him at the altar before the golden calf.

This very same tension arose time and time again in the history of Israel, as the Hebrew people encountered the religious rites of their pagan neighbors. The-God-with-his-people often did not seem as real or as solid to them as the idols of the pagans. And each time the people yielded to the temptation, God raised up prophets to retell the story of the Covenant, to reaffirm his promise to Abraham to be the-God-with-his-people, and to call the people back, back to fidelity to the dream.

When the people put their faith in wealth, position, power or pleasure, prophets were raised up to proclaim the Word of God in their midst, and to remind them that to worship the-God-with-his-people required of them a certain lifestyle—a lifestyle that would be a *sign* that God was truly with them. They were to care for widows and orphans; they were to deal justly with one another; they were to be compassionate to the strangers in their midst, for *only then* would their God become visible.

5. And so there was always a small group who tried to remain faithful to the dream and keep it alive—the Remnant of Israel. It was from this remnant that The Man came. For Jesus was not only born into and bred on that great tradition of the Hebrew people, he incarnated it, making the-God-with-his-people for the first time fully visible and inaugurating the Reign of God, the Coming of the Kingdom.

6. For centuries, the Jews and their ancestors had been the laughing stock of the ancient world. Their neighbors always thought them strange because they carried around the Ark of the Covenant and thought that God actually dwelt with them. Now after centuries of such ridicule, their faith was at long last validated as the Word became flesh and dwelt among us. But the misunderstanding did not cease, not even among the disciples.

After being with him for years, Philip walked up to Jesus one day and asked, "Lord, when are you going to show us the Father?" And Jesus said, "Philip, you're looking at him; the Father and I are one." But in saying that Jesus was revealing not only who he was, but also who we are. For Jesus was saying to

Philip that God is not to be found outside of humankind, but *within,* in the intimacy and togetherness of human and divine, promised and foretold in the Covenant, effected and realized in the Lord Jesus, and present in each one of us when we truly walk with him in faith.

So for the first time, the secret was fully revealed in and by the Lord. God is human not only in Christ Jesus, but is human in each one of us and was human from the very beginning, only no one would believe him when he tried to reveal it. With the coming of Jesus, we know definitively where God is. He is, where he has always been, with, among, and in his people, especially in our noblest parts where justice and charity dwell. *That* is the Good News of the Gospel, and the implementation of that truth is what Scripture calls the Reign of God or the Coming of the Kingdom.

7. Up and down the dusty roads of Palestine, Jesus took every opportunity to proclaim the Coming of the Kingdom to all who would listen. Just being with him caused people to experience a healing presence. They felt freer, walked taller, thought nobler, sang more joyfully, and were happier and more alive than they had ever been before. But that is always what happens when one encounters the God-with-his-people.

Jesus gave himself so completely to this mission that he made enemies among those who claimed to believe in the God of Abraham but whose lifestyles contradicted that claim. In any case, they plotted to get him and finally betrayed him into the hands of those who held the power of life or death in the state. But Jesus remained faithful to the dream to the end, proclaiming, "Father, forgive them they know not what they do. They know not who I am. They know not who they are."

8. Many in those days thought that the death of Jesus would mark the end of the story, but of course it was only a new beginning. The secret was now out. The Reign of God had begun, but it could only come to fullness if that secret were revealed anew in each generation. Jesus of Nazareth was murdered, but he rose in glory and the Spirit of the risen Lord was poured forth on the world so that in every age there would be at least a remnant who believed in the dream and were faithful to it,

incarnating it anew in their lives thus making the Kingdom more fully come.

9. God had promised Abraham that he would be the father of a great people, more numerous than the sands of the seashore or the stars of the heavens. With the first Pentecost, it was time for Yahweh, the Faithful One, to begin fulfilling that part of the promise. The dream and the message were to be spread beyond Israel to the nations. The apostles, aflame with the Spirit, began to move out to the nations of the world, Thomas getting as far as India, Peter and John to the center of their world—Imperial Rome. But it was the great labors of Paul of Tarsus that foretold the shape of things to come.

Never having met Jesus of Nazareth, Paul encountered the risen Lord on the road to Damascus and received his call and commission to bring the Good News to the Gentiles. The God of Abraham, Isaac and Jacob, the God of Israel had revealed in Jesus that he was the-God-with-ALL-his people. Israel was not his sole habitation. He lived and was present in all of humankind. In the past, Israel had been the *sign* of that truth to all the world. Now the Church, the New Israel, was to assume that time-honored role.

10. The litany of the Apostles of the Nations is a long one and marks a glorious page in our story: St. James to Spain; St. Patrick to Ireland; St. Remigius to France; St. Boniface to Germany; St. Gregory to England; St. Ansgar to Scandinavia; Sts. Cyril and Methodius to the Slavs; St. Stephen to Hungary; St. Hyacinth to Poland; St. Francis Xavier to the Indies and Japan—to mention only a few. And always excitement and zeal were generated as Jesus the Christ was preached and the secret of the God-with-all-his-people revealed.

Thanks to the Spirit and the labors of these great Apostles of the Nations, the faith and the dream took deep root in the peoples of Europe. At times the rich and the powerful would play politics with the dream, but the faith was woven into the very fabric of the lives of the common people, especially the poor. They sensed its value because it affirmed their dignity and called on them to do great things for the Lord. It offered them not only the hope that their lives could be transformed, but the way and the means of doing it. And so in every nation, there was always a remnant who remained faithful and dreamed of a better day.

11. When in the fullness of time, a land of freedom and equality was, by the grace of God, fashioned across the seas, it fired the hearts and the imaginations of many. From every nation the immigrants came, selling all they had to book passage, clutching what they could carry, their eyes bright with the dream. They came, like Abraham of old, leaving homeland and family behind but strong in faith and eager to plant that faith for the first time in the rich soil of freedom. They trusted the God-with-all-his-people to bring forth from that union of faith and freedom a rich harvest, a transformed people, a new world.

We are the fruit of that harvest. We are the children of that dream!

Our Faith

1. Proud of our story and wishing to keep faith with this sacred heritage, we feel obliged to rise as a people and to say that *we do not believe in God,* that mythical being who sits on a throne in a far-off perfect land. Nor do we believe in the Monster-God, who lies in wait to punish us for mistakes and crimes.

Our God is totally different. We proclaim him to be the God of Abraham, Isaac, Jacob, Moses and of Jesus, Yahweh, God with us, his people. We believe that he who fashioned us abides with us, walks, suffers and dreams with us. He is the Faithful One who never, never abandons us; he is our Father.

2. We shout out that God, far from merely tolerating our flesh, our passions, our weaknesses, is one of us, our own flesh and blood, Jesus the Christ: the best proof that God loves us and is with us—the final revelation that God has no other home, no other family, no other lover than ourselves.

3. We raise our voices to proclaim that the murdered Jesus is alive and lives in us, sharing his Spirit with his followers, the Spirit that makes us clean and new and glad and hopeful, the Spirit who empowers us to abhor and reject the obscenity of our present world and dream of another world in which human beings will be truly equal, where all will be treated with fairness and

kindness, where there will be no more lust, abuse or domination among us.

4. We announce to the world that we are the disciples of the Lord Jesus, assembled from the four corners of the earth, called to be the *sign* of God's presence and plan, Israel, history's most significant people. With sorrow we accuse ourselves and our world of perverting the plan of God. But joyfully we pledge our lives and fortunes to the coming of his kind of world—the Kingdom of God.

5. We say that we believe it so strongly that we shall do all in our power to live it now. We will be one in love; there will be no differences among us, neither male nor female, black nor white, workers or professional, rich nor poor.

6. We believe in the God of Freedom who wills that his people not be crippled by fear or guilt. Therefore, we have no doubt at all that having been forgiven by the gracious love of God, we are empowered to forgive one another, to heal one another, so we may truly walk together.

7. Because the Lord has called us by name, and because we have offered our lives to his cause, we know that we shall live forever, not alone as individuals, nor as Catholics, nor even as Christians, no, with all our brothers and sisters, when all the clouds will have been chased away, when evil's icy grip on our hearts will have been broken, when our present pain and agony will have been transformed into peace, when we shall enjoy forever in common union the ecstasy of faithful love.

Reflections on the Proclamations

In the four years since *Our Story* and *Our Faith* were first proclaimed, they have been shared with hundreds of people, primarily in the Chicago area. As proclamation statements they have rarely, if ever, been the subject of close study or analysis. You just don't do that to "proclamations." All but those with fundamentalist leanings seem to have found them helpful, refreshing, and even inspiring, but they seem content just to have heard them. Grateful that there were people who took the time to produce a contemporary proclamation of the faith and share it

with them, they seldom pursued the obviously radical implica-
tions of either statement.

Our Faith has had great impact because as a contemporary "creed" it fills a desperate need of believers that they be able
occasionally to profess their Christian faith and commitment
publicly in other than the highly metaphysical language of the
Council of Nicea (325 A.D.) that they don't really understand.
Even in its English version, one can scarcely say that the Nicene
Creed is in the vernacular.

It is fairly obvious that the model chosen for *Our Story*
was the very one used so often by the writers of Scripture. They
take a particular people with a particular history and they use
certain real events in that history in order to mount a dream and
tell the story of God's presence to that people as revealed in their
experience. In *Our Story* the emergence of the United States as
the "land of the free" is seen as a decisive moment (Time II) in
Yahweh's constant endeavor to form a "free" people. This
allows the American Dream to be looked at as in continuity with
the whole Judaeo-Christian tradition, i.e., with the ancient call to
freedom experienced by Israel in Abraham, Moses, and the other
prophets and as experienced by Christians in the incarnation of
the Kingdom in Jesus of Nazareth and his call, as risen Lord, for
that Kingdom to ever more fully come.

By design, *Our Story* ends without bringing us totally
up-to-date. Its final words to us are to remind us who we are, and
on which dream we American Christians have been bred. It stops
short of facing the obvious contradictions Christians in America
today feel as the dream of the Reign of God collides head on with
a secularized American Dream no longer having anything to do
with "incarnation" or God's presence among us. *Our Story* is
primarily concerned with so describing our past that it poses a
challenge to us with regard to our present and our future. The
implied question of *Our Story* is this: If in God's plan there is
always to be a "remnant" who remains faithful to the dream,
who makes up the true remnant in our country today? Where are
we to find them? How are we to recognize them?

Many are uncomfortable with this because they think it
smacks of a triumphal elitism. To talk as if God forms a special
people in every age seems to imply that they are privileged or

special. (Recall Vatican II's unfortunate terminology in calling Catholics "the privileged of the privileged.") The truth is the "remnant" is called to *service,* not privilege; they are not the "saved" but are called to be servants of both the "saved" and "unsaved," if any such there be. They are not the recipients of special gifts, but are to be themselves God's own "gift" *to the world.*

They are not to embrace the Gospel message and its imperatives so as to be better than others, or to judge others, but because they have once again heard the cry of the Lord: "form me a people, my people!" A People who, being a *sign* of the Kingdom which is to come, will reveal to the world that life is stronger than death; faith more fruitful than either doubt or religion; that hope is brighter than despair; and that love, not selfishness, is built to last forever. A People who will support and confirm the noblest aspirations and endeavors of all persons of good will. In short, a People who can convince our world of God's love and of his redeeming presence to all of humankind.

CHAPTER SIX

Breaking Camp Again

One important and sometimes bitter lesson Catholics have learned from their experiences over the past 30 years is that Christians are not so much a people of the Promised Land as we are an Exodus people. An Exodus people have a tradition of liberation and freedom, and so the Jews of Jesus' time were offended and resented it when he told them that he had come to *really* set them free. They responded angrily: "We are descendants of Abraham and have never been in bondage to anyone. How is it that you say: 'You shall be *made* free'?" (John 8:33)

A clear indication that they had lost touch with what their Exodus freedom tradition really meant! As *Our Story* clearly proclaims: "With the Exodus was born that beautiful tradition of the Hebrew people, to which we also are heirs, that *they were not only called to freedom themselves, but were called to be the very sign of God's liberating presence in the world*" (3). What they failed to understand is that the Exodus experience is not guaranteed for any people by their past history and traditions, and that the march out of bondage and the subsequent long trek in the desert will never be over for us until the Kingdom comes fully. For those who walk with the Lord, Exodus is just as much a present experience as it is a glorious event in their past.

Given the human condition, this proves to be a mixed blessing. If we concentrate only on the fact that we ourselves are called to freedom, the Exodus tradition is exhilarating and always ready at hand to motivate us when our own freedom and dignity are in danger. Our enthusiasm for Exodus is noticeably lessened, however, when we look at that tradition in its entirety, as Elizabeth O'Connor does so candidly in *The New Community,* (Harper & Row, 1976, p.18):

> The old in us argues and fights to maintain things as they are, clinging to that which is known and secure and promises protection. We cannot overcome our dependencies and fear, and acquire a whole new liberating attitude, and at the same time keep

89

everything as it is. If something new comes into being in us—if *metanoia* happens, something old has had to make way for it. . . . Old positions are given up and one's life becomes unified around the new, which then becomes the place of God's rest. *But camp will have to be broken again for we are the People of the Exodus.* The long trek out of bondage is not over.

We resist change, even when it is liberating, because the old in us, which has become second nature and our chosen way of being present to the world, will not easily yield its place to the new. That, of course, is an euphemism, it is *we* who will not yield to the new. As Ludwig Feuerbach once put it: "What has once existed will not be denied the right to exist forever; *what was once good, claims to be good for all times.*" For Christians, the conflict is always between this natural conservative inclination at our center, and our Exodus vocation, i.e., the call to be "a new creation" in Christ.

The temptation is always to go back. It is a basic law of human life that as we pass from stage to stage in our development we are frightened by the challenge of having to once again readjust and adapt to the new. The young girl wants to remain a tomboy and not become a woman, the middle-aged male wants to remain a swinger and not accept the task of discovering the meaning of his "maleness" apart from sexual machismo. Faced with such decisive moments in our personal journeys, the temptation is always to refuse to move on, to refuse to master new ways of being who we are in the world, and to return to patterns of life which served us so well in the past. At such moments, the challenge is always to have the courage to move forward. Each time "we break camp" the issue is once again in doubt. For breaking camp means only that we will once again be on the move; it does not guarantee that we shall continue our journey. We are always free to choose to return to Egypt.

Our Lost Spirituality

In the preceding chapters, I have been at pains to argue that the movement from "religion" to "faith" is a classic example of the Exodus experience. For contemporary Catholics, Vatican II marks an institutional "breaking of camp" unheralded in the history of the Church. In its wake, everyone is on the move, some walking away from the Church, some opting to return to Egypt, and others accepting the challenge of an uncertain future with the Lord in the desert. The cost in terms of human anguish has been enormous. But then Exodus was never meant to be painless; there is no growth or liberation-salvation without tears.

Of the many pains endured by the Catholic community over the past decade and a half, there seems to be one which marks the lives of adult Catholics regardless of where they are coming from theologically. *We have lost our spirituality.* In those first years after Vatican II, under the heady influence of the feeling of liberation, change, and creativity, we were blissfully unaware of that fact. But as the years after Vatican II have stretched into a second decade, we are beginning to own up to our deep sense of loss. The temptation, as usual, is to rush back to the tried and true spiritualities of the past, especially when we see them so effectively lived in others, e.g., the Catholic Charismatics and Mother Teresa of Calcutta. When it is practiced with zeal and to perfection, traditional spirituality still is very attractive to our pre-Vatican II hearts and makes us all the more keenly aware of our loss. Suddenly, we find ourselves hankering after a return to Egypt.

If we have learned anything in the past two decades, our experience has taught us that we cannot go on indefinitely without an identifiable spirituality. We do all right without one for the short term, but our present sense of loss teaches us that it will not work for the long haul. Realizing that, many have decided to go back to a spirituality of the past rather than attempt to go on without one. But should we go back, many of us will discover another painful truth about human life: *There is, generally, no going home again.*

We have all gone to class reunions, returned to the old neighborhood, gathered with friends from the past, and though there may be rare exceptions, most often we are painfully reminded of the fact that time does not stand still, that people and attitudes do change, and that nostalgia is one of the most unrealistic of human passions. This is not to deny that there will be some among us for whom spiritual nostalgia can be a source of life. But it is to affirm that for many others of us, it is impossible to return to the "religious" practices of our youth as life-giving. For those of us in the second group, we must either learn to live with our present sense of loss, or we must attempt to articulate and practice a spirituality that answers our needs in the present and yet is recognizable as *an authentic way of walking with the Lord in faith.*

In my own life, this has not been an easy task. In the late 70's I began to experience a deep sense of loss. I mourned my lost spirituality, and felt that there was something missing in my life. While in that state of mind, I tried a little experiment. I decided to return to the devotions and practices of my pre-Vatican II life which had been so life-giving. I reasoned that at least I would have the consolation of knowing that I was doing something constructive and not merely drifting aimlessly with the tides of change.

I began to attend Mass several times during the week, to do more spiritual reading, to say the rosary every day, and even to say the major parts of the Divine Office several days a week. All of those things had, in the past, given me a feeling of closeness to God and sustained me in my spiritual journey. A return to them was bound to ease this feeling of laxity and of something important missing from my life, or so I thought. For three months, I went on with the experiment, but I realized early on that it was no good for me. What had once been vital and the source of spiritual energy was no longer so. It all seemed so terribly artificial and contrived. It was then I learned the truth about myself. I was one of those who could not go back. I had changed.

Now there are those who will immediately conclude that I was going through some "dark night of the soul," which is a normal stage in everyone's spiritual development. But I had long ago read and studied about this phenomenon, and I was convinced that that was not what I was now experiencing. The dark night of the soul is characterized by the fact that one gets no solace or spiritual consolation from doing what one knows God wants one to do, but because it is what God wants, one continues to do it. My experience was different. I found no life in returning to the pre-Vatican II practices and devotions because I was not at all convinced that that was what God wanted. I interpreted that to mean that my experience was revealing to me what Yahweh long ago revealed to the Hebrews: "It is love that I desire, not sacrifice, and knowledge of God rather than holocausts" (Hosea 6:6). I then remembered another experience I had had almost a decade before, when I had come to the same conclusion.

It began one day when I was reflecting on what it means for God to be our Father. Naturally, since I am myself a father of four sons and two daughters, I tried to understand that revelation in terms of my own experiences as a father. I asked myself, what is it that turns me on most as a father? What is it that joys me, makes my heart soar in song, and convinces me that Julian of Norwich spoke Gospel when she said: "All will be well, and all will be well, and all manner of things will be well." Whatever that turned out to be, that would be what God as Father wants most from us.

I searched my experiences for the answer. I recognized that though I dearly liked being affirmed by my children, I was most uncomfortable when they overdid it. I was not at peace when they kept saying: "Dad, you're really great!" "Pop, you're super!" etc. What turned me on most was not their words at all. I realized that when my children lived up to the ideals we had shared in the family, when they did what love required under the circumstances, I began to puff up like a blimp, not with pride you understand, but with joy. It was at such moments that I felt most affirmed as their father. Now if Jesus has revealed to us that God is our Father, then the same must be true of him, at least in an analogous way.

Some weeks later, I was participating in a program of formation in one of the local parishes. One of the participants asked me a question, and in answering it suddenly everything came together. She asked: "Do you ever say 'Praise the Lord'?" I looked at her in utter amazement. She was obviously a charismatic of the more fundamentalist type. She had an obscenely large sterling silver dove on a large silver ring around her neck, representing the Holy Spirit, and throughout the program she had kept interjecting aloud the ejaculation "Praise the Lord."

I asked her for some clarification. "Do you mean do I

ever utter those exact three words?'' ''Yes, that's what I mean,''
she replied. I admitted that I was not in the habit of using that
phrase. She then leaned forward to give me her best counsel,
''Well, if you would just say those words, everything would be
all right with your life.'' I looked into her face. She was
completely serious. Knowing that she was not capable of understanding a word of what I would say, I ended our conversation
with: ''You see, if I am truly walking with the Lord and living my
life as a sign of his presence, I *am* the praise of the Lord. So there
is really no reason for me to be saying it all the time.''

The lesson is clear. As *Our Story* affirmed (4), the praise
and worship of the Lord are not primarily a matter of words, they
are a matter of lifestyle. Therein lies a crucial difference between
religion and incarnational faith. If we are unmindful of that fact,
we are bound to misjudge our own children. While it may be true
that many of them find no meaning in Sunday worship, and hence
can be judged irreligious, it is also true that a significant number
of them live lives that praise the Lord more than the lives we lead.
Spirituality is not a matter of religious practices, it is a matter of
living a certain kind of life. This life has built into it regular
behaviour patterns that put one in touch with the God who, to
prove his desire for intimacy with us, has incarnated himself in
our very life and history. A final example from my own parenting
puts this truth in stark relief.

One of my sons got himself involved helping teenagers
struck down my muscular dystrophy. Usually the victims don't
live beyond their early twenties, and their families minister to
them 24 hours a day, seven days a week without respite. My son
founded a non-profit organization which took these young people
away from their families for weekends. It gave the parents some
little relief and was one of the rare times the dystrophic teenagers
could be away from mother and dad and be with their peer group.
A precious ''gift'' to both parents and teenager alike! The
organization would load ten or 11 of the dystrophic people in
vans, wheelchairs and all, and go on camp-outs, rock concerts,
etc. The goal was to give them some semblance of a normal
teenage social life. When these events occurred, it required
tremendous energy and time-commitment from the group. Eigh-
teen and twenty hour days were not uncommon.

It was on the occasion of one such event, that on a Sunday morning the family was heading off to Mass. As we were getting ready to leave, my son came down sleepy-eyed. I almost automatically said: ''I don't suppose you're going to Church today?'' I had really meant it to be a request for information. I wanted to know whether we were to wait for him while he rushed to get ready. Unfortunately, it came out sounding very sarcastic. He turned on me and taught me a valuable lesson for which I remain in his debt. He said angrily: ''Don't shrink me, Pop. I was in Church all day yesterday. Where the hell were you?''

The new spiritualities which are aborning are all going to be much more incarnational and much less religious than those on which we were raised. If we fail to understand that, we shall continue to judge that our children have rejected God and shall worry unnecessarily about their spiritual well-being. We must recognize that our children have no love for Egypt, because they have been called to make the deserts bloom. If we deem them godless, it is only because we ourselves continue to entertain a religious image of God and have failed to really come to know the God of *our* fathers. It is *we* and not they who have lost our spirituality.

Prayer and Spirituality

For those who identify spirituality with prayer, no more proof is needed that we have lost our spirituality than the fact that we don't pray as much as we used to. This opinion is held by those among us who whenever we ''break camp'' make a bee line for Egypt. To justify their impoverished outlook they find it necessary to make people feel guilty because they no longer pray the way they once did. We should be grateful they don't.

Much, if not all, of our praying was of ''religious'' inspiration having little or nothing to do with faith or was the result of religious hang-ups. We had been urged to fill every moment with what looked like prayer. An impossible bit of counsel which either caused us to despair of ever having an authentic spiritual life, or forced us to adopt behaviour patterns which bear a marked resemblance to the obsessive or compulsive behaviour of the emotionally disturbed. The truth, as Eugene

Kennedy observed, is that "most people pray more than they think and better than they imagine."

What makes a discussion of "prayer" so difficult is that it does not designate a single thing, but stands instead for a whole spectrum of human realities. No matter how far along a person develops in the spiritual life, she usually retains vestiges of her more primitive prayer experiences. That is to say, in moments of stress and profound emotion it is natural for us humans to revert to the "religious" prayer practices we have long given up because we have simply grown beyond them. That is one of the knee-jerk reflex actions of the spiritual life. Our prayer life exists in each of us on three recognizable levels which are especially worthy of note.

Psychological Prayer   A human person is a precarious balance of organic and symbolic needs. If these needs are not met, dehumanization can be the result. We all need some measure of alone time (Time II), wherein we move away from the everyday-ness of our lives, turn our attention away from such concerns and pull ourselves together. This sort of integration is more and more essential in our frenetic world. Some people set aside time for prayer in order to meet these very human needs. Praying on this level actually induces a better quality of consciousness and provides us with energy for action (we hope good and noble action) which would not otherwise be available to us. Of course, one need not pray to achieve such results, as is clear from the tremendous success of TM (transcendental meditation). On this level of our lives, *psychological prayer* is therapeutic and makes a helpful contribution to our personal development.

Religious Prayer   But not all our needs are met by psychic integration. Even the most well integrated of personalities eventually comes face to face with finitude, and the meaning of human life in the light of the inevitable approach of death. Humankind generally copes with this dimension of existence either by repressing the anxiety stemming from our recognized finitude, covering it over with some form of self-deception or, by facing our finitude squarely and freely accepting it, we transcend outward to the Diety thus anchoring our mutable limited existence in an immutable and infinite God.

It is on this level that we have what we normally take to be *the* model of prayer. Religious prayer certainly relates a person to God, but the relationship is tenuous at best since it occurs across the unbridgeable chasms of finite and infinite. The infinite God is a perfect religious object because we can nourish ourselves in his greatness and power. We stand in awe and are often drawn into hymns of praise and adoration which mark not only his greatness but our creatureliness. Prayer on this level redeems our finitude but it cannot redeem us because it lacks the proper openness and intimacy. *Religious prayer* is the invention of Adam I and Eve I to help cope with finitude. As such, it bears all the marks of self-interest and power and is generally too pragmatically human to be the paradigm of what prayer is at its best.

The Prayer of Faith   Religious prayer has such a firm hold on us that we find prayer on the level of incarnational faith to be completely unbelievable and certainly unachievable. And our instincts are quite correct. Prayer at its best is not something *we* achieve; it is a gift. The *prayer of faith* is born of the Covenant wherein the Lord God pledged everlasting intimacy with humankind. It is the voice of Adam II and Eve II in response to that pledge. In the light of the Covenant, there is no chasm between finite and infinite. People are called to intimacy with the Lord God who breathed life into them and who is close at hand. To the prophet Micah he had said: "Only this do I, the Lord of Yahweh, ask of you, that you act justly, love tenderly and walk humbly with your God." (Micah 6:8) The *prayer of faith* is simply what we say in intimacy on such a stroll.

For those who would like to consult a fuller account of prayer and the spiritual life, I would recommend as essential Matthew Fox, *On Becoming a Musical Mystical Bear* (Harper and Row, 1972) and Eugene Kennedy, *A Contemporary Meditation on Prayer* (Thomas More, 1975).

Our Flight From Intimacy

Whatever else may be said about a return to Egypt, it is essentially a flight from intimacy.

We have seen that it is characteristic of Adam and Eve I that they *confront* their world and the people in it, putting their relationships with them to some self-serving purpose. It is the mark of Adam and Eve II that they do not so much confront others as they *encounter* the world and its people in the hope of thereby meeting God in intimacy. In the wide range of human relationships, confrontation though more prevalent is also a much more superficial way for people to touch one another. Confrontation requires only that degree of involvement with the other that enables me to manipulate her and put her to use in my own interests. Encounter, on the other hand, is a more profound and deeper sharing of the very self with another; it is characterized by graciousness on both sides. Intimacy is, in the end, a gift given to another and not something the other can claim by right.

In every era there are certain catch words which are used to sum up for Christians some particular aspect of their struggle for an adequate spiritual life. It is no accident that in our own time that the word is "encounter." It is considered so important by Christians in today's world that two significant examples of "Church" have incorporated it into their very titles: *M*arriage *E*ncounter, and *T*eens *E*ncounter *C*hrist, (*ME* and *TEC*).

If we define a spirituality of faith as a patterned style of behavior whereby we seek to put and maintain ourselves in touch with God by relating to him in intimacy, we can perhaps better understand the right-headedness of the current stress on encounter, which is to say, intimacy. *Without "encounter" all spiritualities are inevitably reduced to nothing more than religious confrontation,* confrontations in which either God would try to subject us to his will, or what is equally comic, we would attempt to bend him to ours. A God-relation is confrontational and hence religious whenever either of these two things occur. Little reflection is required to show that such a relation is incompatible both with the Lord Yahweh of Adam and Eve II, and with the Father as Jesus reveals him to us.

Despite this fact, most of the language describing our relationship to God is blatantly confrontational. We are told that we are to be "subject" to his will, that we are to be obedient and keep his commandments, that as creatures we are beholden and obliged to him as Creator, and finally, we must render him proper adoration, praise, worship, and service as divine king. Not one word about intimacy! Even when we try to speak of him in terms of love, we manage to make him seem somehow remote from us: "If you love me, keep my commandments" and "God so loved the world . . . he sent his son . . ."

Our tradition is filled with such things, and so we are paralyzed and unable to make the move from confrontation (religion) to encounter (faith) because we see that as betrayal. The truth is, betrayal comes from our unwillingness to discern in that tradition what is of religion and what of incarnational faith. Unaware of that and wishing to remain faithful, we continue to say not only that God himself *wants* us subject to his will, but go on the proclaim to the whole world that the norm of true sanctity consists in nothing less.

The relationship between God and ourselves is not a contest of wills, i.e., it is not confrontational. It is an invitation to loving encounter, intimacy, love, communion, and oneness, as Chapters 14 and 15 of the Gospel of John so beautifully attest. But while it is true that this truth is clearly contained in the Scriptures, it is also true that it is often overlooked there in favor of the many religious elements with which it is made to coexist. I am convinced myself that the truth about our God-relation is more readily available to us not in the Book, but in life.

Life itself inexorably teaches us the truth of the call to intimacy with God, with one another and the world in unambiguous terms. That should not prove surprising, however, because as we have seen, the Scriptures themselves arose from the lived experiences of believing people. We fail to learn the lesson that our lived experience clearly reveals because of our unwillingness to give up our religious prejudices. We continue to be held hostage to the "religious" elements of Scripture and our tradition. We ignore the God of life in favor of a religious idol. The words of the prophet Jeremiah continue to stand as a reproach to all such "religious" accounts of God: "My people are fools, they know me not. They are senseless children having no understanding of me" (Jer. 4:22).

I suppose that there will be those who think that "encounter" and "intimacy" are merely psychological categories that happen to be very fashionable just now. Once this personalist fad passes, everything will return to normal. But those believers who have experienced loving encounter and intimacy have discovered that these are more than just elements in sound mental health. They are the very stuff of salvation.

Moments of encounter and intimacy are very special time (*kairos* or Time II); they are unique and can never really be repeated. The reason is that persons involved in genuine encounters are profoundly changed by them. When they encounter the next time, they are different by virtue of their prior encounters and so the new encounter is as unique as they are. Work time, recreation time etc. are linear time (*chronos* or Time I), which means they *can* be repeated and that they can be "time wasted" or "time used up." Only relationship-building time and alone time, that is, the time of encountering my fellow human beings or God in intimacy (Time II) can be "saved" from oblivion. That is because it is the only time that can become an integral part of who I am and hence be carried over into the present *in my very person*. The time of intimate encounter is very sacred time (*kairos*) and constitutes the heart of any authentic spirituality. It is the salvation time of our lives.

A harried mother of a large family who is overwhelmed by all she must do to prepare for the Christmas holidays might well be heard to say in her fatigue: "It's Christmas, *again*." That word "again" is always the tip-off that we are concerned with linear time, not with relationship or salvation time. Should a spouse say wearily, "Oh, it's time to have sexual relations *again*," we would have a sure indication that he or she looked on the act as obligatory and part of, you'll excuse the expression, the "marriage debt."

If the mother were really into the warm relationships and family reunions, which Christmas always precipitates, rather than the impossible work burden placed upon her, she would be more apt to say something like this: "I can't wait until Christmas." If the spouse viewed sexual relations as an important element in the building of a relationship rather than as a husbandly or wifely work to be done, he or she might have said what Yahweh said to Adam II, "Darling, look what I've got for you!" The word "again" would never occur.

The same is true with Christianity. Real believers aren't

overheard saying: "It's Sunday; we've got to go to Mass *again*." or "As a Christian I have no alternative but to love my neighbor *again*." Such things make no sense to people of faith. Nor would we ever hear from such people the complaint, "Damn, it's time to break camp *again!*" "You mean we have to go out into the desert and relive the Exodus *again?*" Whenever we talk like that, we are already well on our way back to Egypt.

Our Lack of Vision

We are all familiar with irony as a figure of speech. It occurs when what we mean is the exact opposite of the words we say. If a Jew were to say: "I think Baal and Moloch are terrific gods!" or "I think Hitler was simply marvelous," we would expect to recognize that she meant exactly the opposite by the tone and inflection with which she delivered those lines. Of course, sometimes the tone is neutral and the inflection absent, and then we are not quite sure if we should take the person seriously or if she is speaking ironically. But irony is not merely a property of speech patterns. It is a basic characteristic of life and reality itself. *Things are not what they seem.* Any religion worthy of the name will attempt to underscore that fact, but as a "faith," Judaeo-Christianity is more essentially ironic than any of the world's religions. Consider that for the Christian

the God who seems absent is intimately present
the God who is divine is really human
what looks like bread and wine, isn't
the poor are rich
the weak are strong
loss is really gain
self-sacrifice is victory
time that is useless (Time II) is most valuable
he who would lose his life will save it
the dead aren't really dead, they live

to mention only a few of the ironies of our faith.

The fact is that *if things were simply as they appear, humankind would have no need of a spirituality.* But human life is completely ironic, and because we sense that is so, each of us has the need to make the effort to see reality as it really is, i.e., ironically. We might define spirituality as our attempt at an altered state of consciousness, wherein we come to *see* the normally invisible and *hear* the normally inaudible dimensions of life. To lack a spirituality, or to have no time for one, is to be stuck with things as they appear, which would be to miss the point of it all.

Missing the point of it all is nothing new for humankind. If the meaning of life were on the surface of things, if it were revealed to us in the same way as a sunset, or the smell of newly mown hay, or the song of the robin, then the meaning of it all would be readily accessible to the Adam and Eve I in each of us. It would be just one more observable fact about the world; there would be no mystery and nothing ironic about human life. In that case, the human sciences would be adequate to the task of delivering the secret of life. But life's meaning is not to be found on its surface; it lies deeper. If it were not for the fact that there is an Adam and Eve II in each of us as well, we would not even be aware of that fact. Only the Adam and Eve II part of us is "unselfed" enough to see and hear what escapes the self-interested counterparts. While the Adam and Eve I in us lives out its life in linear time, the Adam and Eve II searches for intimacy and relationships, thereby piercing the irony and discovering the salvation time of life.

Throughout this book, I have been especially concerned with one particular irony, namely, that Christianity, which looks like a religion, really isn't. But to *see* that requires a deep and profound spirituality available only to the Adam and Eve II in us. I have no illusions, therefore, that this book can impart that insight. We don't learn such truths by reading books, but rather by getting more and more in touch with our deepest experiences. For it is the risen Lord who reveals his truth there, opening our eyes to the invisible and our ears to the inaudible. The heart and soul of that revelation, as I am now convinced, is that *intimacy is redemptive*. It is to that *central truth of faith* that we can now finally turn.

CHAPTER SEVEN

Redemptive Intimacy

Salvation invisibly accompanies us along our way. God is always very near to a man through the various ages of life; but man's eyes are closed and he is not quite aware of it, he does not look closely enough, for he desires, he hankers and is so busy.

Just as one can tell time by the shadow an object casts, so can one determine a person's maturity according to how close to him he thinks God is. Youth and adulthood run their course; it is not until evening comes and days decline that one understands that God is closer than all else, although one has not appreciated that fact.

Soren Kierkegaard

It may be very well and good for us to say, as we did earlier, that since God created both Adam and Eve I and Adam and Eve II, we must find a way to integrate and harmonize both facets of our personality. If we but live long enough, however, life teaches us that this really means that we must search for and make a concerted effort to live up to the Adam and Eve II in us. That is something which can only be learned from experience.

On the other hand, we require little or no instruction to live up to the Adam and Eve I in ourselves, because most of us seem able to do that instinctively and naturally. Redemption, as I hope to show in this chapter, is not achieved by our forward surges as Adam and Eve I, but rather by our humble yielding to the other as Adam and Eve II. *Redemption is just another name for learning the lessons of intimacy.* Adam and Eve I are incapable of learning those lessons because they are constitutionally unable to yield, or let go. It is because of the predominance of the Adam and Eve I in our lives that the most difficult lesson in life for us is always learning to let go. Many *never* learn it. If we are to succeed, it will only be because we have finally "owned" and "responded to" the Adam and Eve II dimensions of our humanity.

One would have thought that Christianity, which is based on "incarnation", i.e., *the intimacy between the Lord God and all of humankind,* was ideally suited to facilitate that learning process. Alas, not so. For far too many Christians, the Jesus-story has been turned into a morality play in which his coming is interpreted as redeeming us from our sins, and the Christian vocation reduced to the insipid call to keep the commandments, to be "morally good," or save one's own soul. In such a view, life's central lesson of yielding is understood simply as obedience to the commandments, and God is said to have become human in order to save us from our sins.

Because that view of the matter is the dominating surface view of the New Testament itself, Christians are reluctant to allow their lived experience to teach them the lessons of intimacy. Having interpreted the Incarnation as a morality play, they spend their energies in avoiding sin, not realizing that they are called to much more—to intimacy. So the Incarnation, which should have been our greatest clue to the truth, became something of a detriment, when interpreted religiously, to our coming to really know the Lord God and appreciate his ways of working in our world.

Fortunately, not all Christians have been taken in by the "religious" account of Christianity. In every age, there has always been a "remnant" who somehow came to a different understanding of the Christian enterprise. Perhaps no one struggled more consistently with the conflict between religion and faith in his own life than the great St. Athanasius, for 45 years the Bishop of Alexandria, 328-373 A.D. Because of his profound belief in and commitment to the Incarnation, his personal struggle gave birth to a statement which lies at the very heart of incarnational faith. "God became man, so that man might become divine" (*De Incarnatione Verbi*, 54).

In our own times, Vatican II gave that same truth expression in its *Decree on the Missions:* "Therefore, the Son of God walked the ways of a true incarnation that he might make men sharers in the divine nature" (*Ad Gentes,* 3). Christianity is not, after all, a morality play; it is an account of the divinization of the human race by means of redemptive intimacy between the Lord God and humankind as incarnated in Jesus. Only if that is

truly the case are the two great commandments of love intelligi-
ble. Each of us could keep all ten of the commandments, all of
the time, and still not be divinized or transformed. Yet it is *our*
transformation and divinization that constitute the Lord's dream,
the Coming of the Kingdom. The truth is that intimacy is both a
human and a Gospel imperative; we can be neither human nor
Christian without it. *There is no use our any longer pretending to
love everyone in general (Christian charity) if we are not willing to
risk being intimate with someone in particular.*

Intimacy Considered

At our center, we all share the human condition and are
painfully the same no matter what the other differences between
us. We cope with finitude, failure, advancing age, approaching
death, and in the process come to recognize ourselves as broken
and wounded. We mask that fact most of our waking hours (The
Adam and Eve I in us requires that), but when we cannot sleep·
and are alone in the still of night, we have an irresistible urge to
tear off our masks and reveal our true selves to someone—to
anyone—in the hope that he or she too will unmask and affirm the
solidarity in weakness we all experience. *Our strengths divide
and isolate us; it is in our weaknesses that we are one,* which is
why intimacy is out of the question for Adam and Eve I.

What is it about Adam and Eve I that puts intimacy
beyond their grasp? They live their lives according to what Henri
Nouwen calls the "taking form," by which he means they are
always operating out of a power mode. To sustain that sort of life,
they must be armed against their fellows and one another. They
are constantly on the alert, watching lest they be taken, and
anxious to spot in the other any weakness they might exploit to
their own advantage. They live constantly in a war-emergency
posture; they are not at peace, and so love and intimacy are not
even looked upon as possibilities by them. (See Henri Nouwen,
Intimacy, Fides Press, 1969, especially the revealing second
chapter: "The Challenge To Love" pp. 23-37.)

Those old enough to remember World War II will
understand what I mean when I say that in the "taking form of
existence" love and intimacy are like . . . selling scrap metal to
Japan. For those who can't remember back that far, the same

point might be made by asking why it is that people are so wary of revealing their deepest thoughts. It is because whatever of their deepest selves they reveal in intimacy to others is all too often turned into weaponry and subsequently used against them. Is love, in the end, just an excuse to get the other to reveal intimate things about herself, things which I may use at a later date to get my own way?

Such an assessment of love may strike us as totally cynical, but the fact is that it is in the main accurate. In all of our relations with others we are constantly "making book" on them and storing what we learn for possible future use when that information may be helpful in coping with them when they stand between us and what we want. I imagine it this way. There is a computer in each of our heads that is constantly taking in, classifying, and storing minute bits of seemingly unimportant information about each of the persons we contact. The information thus collected is in itself innocuous enough, but the computer in our head automatically stores it all in the form of weapons for defense.

As humans we do not have horns, or fangs, or claws. Instead, we are endowed with the ability to take any bit of information about the other and to transform it into a weapon capable of wounding and harming her whenever the situation warrants. This defense mechanism, like our heartbeat, works automatically and is not fully under control. We seem to store what we know of the other as weaponry whether we mean to or not. So in interpersonal situations in which the other confronts us, the silos in our brain automatically open up, the missiles rise to the ready, and all we have to do is push the buttons to release them. The construction and deployment of these weapons are automatic and done subconsciously at times, but whether we fire them or not is a matter of conscious human choice.

A husband who really dislikes dancing may see the disappointment in his wife's eyes. He tells her that just because he doesn't like dancing there is no reason for her not to dance. So at parties, though he prefers the conversation at the table, he encourages his wife to participate in dancing. The couple's friends understand and so the wife has no trouble at all finding dance partners. This goes on uneventfully for many years. Then

one fateful evening in the midst of an argumentative contronta-
tion the bunkers in the husband's head open up, the missiles are
aimed, and he makes the tragic mistake of pushing the buttons,
hoping thereby to win the argument and get his way. "You are
nothing but a little tramp. You are always flirting with other men,
and I am so embarrassed at your behaviour in public. It's cheap."

She looks at him stunned. She can't believe what she is
hearing. But he is not finished. He fires off a few more salvos,
mentioning this thing about her dancing with Mr. X two years
ago, and that thing about when she danced with Mr. Y last
month, etc. etc. Totally demolished and with tears in her eyes,
she asks pitifully: "After all these years, is that *really* what you
think of me? Do you really think I'm cheap and a tramp?" The
husband may have won the argument that night, but the harm
done to his relationship with his wife could well be irreparable.

He is not to be criticized because he had all that weaponry
at his disposal. That is an automatic human reflex and an integral
part of our being human; we are all in that position. The tragedy
was that he ever used it. The fact that we are all constantly
"making book" on each other seems to make love and intimacy
an unrealistic ideal. Why in the world would anyone reveal
herself in intimacy knowing full well that what had thus been
revealed would eventually be turned against her? As compulsive
button-pushers, Adam and Eve I avoid intimacy because it poses a
serious threat to their ability to dominate and succeed. Inasmuch as
intimacy arms their adversaries, lessens their power, and decreases
their chances for success, it is far too risky and is to be avoided at
all costs.

Fortunately, that is not the whole story. Another part of us
hungers for intimacy. As we saw in Chapter Four, a life of power
and might may be dignified and mark us off from the animals, but it
does not fully satisfy us because such a self-seeking existence is
not redemptive. It cannot deliver us from our loneliness and
isolation. It does not allow us to be touched by a healing
community, and it does not lead to an intimate encounter with the
Lord God. The Adam and Eve II in us will be satisfied with
nothing less.

There is a helpful clue to all of this from our lived
experience. We have all experienced a wide variety of joys in our

lives. We always experience joy when we possess something truly good for us, or which we take to be good for us. Not all our joys are physical, however. There is an exultation, a gladdening in excess of anything physical, which gives us access to a non-physical world of sunniness without sunlight, of sweet things that have no taste, a world of quiet without inertia, of song without words or music. It is a mysterious kind of joy with no face or figure, no shape or weight, with nothing physical about it other than the fact that it is experienced by someone who is herself physical. As persons we have all had moments like that, moments of a joy indescribable. At such times we can be heard to squeal with delight and exclaim, "In truth, I know not why I am so glad; it heartens me and joys my heart. Yet how I caught it, found it, or came to it, of what stuff it is made, or where it came from, I cannot say. But this I know: I have never been so joyed, never so whole, never so much in touch with what is truly good."

An analysis of such moments invariably reveals that they are the moments of "encounter" (Time II), in which I really cared for someone else, or they really cared for me. To be sure, we truly rejoice in possessing all manner of things that we need for our physical well-being and comfort or want as signs of our worth, but we love those things the way a dog loves its dinner. Such joys arise from "possessing" particular good things. Adam and Eve I know no higher joys than these, the joys of having and holding something good. The indescribable, redemptive human joy does not come from "having" so much as from "giving," nor from "owning" a particular good so much as from encountering and being present to Goodness itself.

Things can be very good, but from the point of view of incarnational faith only persons are the very dwelling place of Goodness itself. Nothing is so like God, nothing is so God-filled as a human person. Small wonder, then that loving things is not as pleasant or joy-filled for us as loving and being loved by persons. To love persons *is* to love God, to love God *is* to love persons (1 John 4:20).

If we don't experience that supreme joy in caring for or being cared for by persons, it can only be because *they and we don't care enough*. And because we don't care enough, we are not only robbed of the supreme joy of life, but are unable to learn that *intimacy redeems,* and so seek our salvation elsewhere. As we examine our experiences in this matter we should ask ourselves this question: Yes or no: Is there any joy equal to the joy of really caring for another, of forgiving, forgetting, of affirming, and loving? The answer of authentic human experience is quite definite on that point: None whatever.

Jesus of Nazareth incarnated that truth. His dream, of the Coming Kingdom or Reign of God, is the continuing incarnation of that truth in all of humankind. Taste and see how good intimacy is! That tasting is not a taste upon the tongue. It is a tasting of something humanly good, of something which is wondrous honey on the tongue and sweet song in the heart. That something is God—as experienced in and through the intimacy of persons. That something *is* redemption, for only intimate encounter can deliver us from our loneliness, isolation, and alienation. Only intimacy heals us by assuaging our doubts about God's forgiveness and empowering us to forgive one another. Only in intimacy do we ''encounter'' the one who makes intimacy possible—the Great Self in whom all being is rooted and finds redemption. If intimacy is not redemptive, then nothing in this life ever can be.

''Religious'' Christians take a different view. They see intimacy as the *result,* not the *cause,* of redemption. It is the cross of Christ that redeems, thus making intimacy possible. They find my account objectionable because no mention is made of the cross. Despite the fact that salvation-redemption is admittedly a mystery, Christians have always felt quite comfortable about their ability to describe it in detail. And why shouldn't they? The New Testament is quite explicit on that point. Indeed, after proclaiming that the ways of God are inscrutable (Rom. 11:33), we, like St. Paul, find no contradiction in immediately thereafter fully explaining them.

The truth is that *all* our attempts at articulating the ways of God to humanity are approximations of human fashioning, as open to misunderstanding as they are revealing. That surely must be said of the ''intimacy-account'' of salvation I am presenting in this chapter. To the degree that it is defective, it stands as an invitation to other Christians to present a still more adequate account from their own experiences. Contrary to what most

Christians think, the same must also be said of the "crucifixion-account" of salvation. Despite the fact that the New Testament is filled with it, it is but one of the many "metaphors" the Scripture writers used to proclaim God's saving actions among us, and despite its prominence in Scripture and subsequent tradition, it is not without serious difficulties of its own.

The Crucifixion Reconsidered

Christians generally agree that Jesus of Nazareth was in fact actually crucified that despite appearances to the contrary, he *freely* laid down his life since no one had the power to take it from him unless he willed it (John 10:18); and that evident in the passion and death of Jesus is the depth of his own and his Father's love for humankind. But the claim that it is by means of his death on the cross that Jesus effected our salvation has always generated problems for Christians, problems that are not really avoided simply by saying that we were redeemed by his life, death, *and* resurrection.

For some time now, it has become customary to speak of the whole "Jesus-event" as salvific, so the problems with the crucifixion are less obvious and less pressing. Yet despite all of the fine and balanced distinctions and nuanced language of the theologians and Scripture scholars, it remains true that most Christians are firmly convinced that we were redeemed on Good Friday by means of Christ's passion and death. Who can fault them? The New Testament seems amazingly clear and single-minded on that point. (See Matt. 26:28; Mark 10:33-34, 45.)

Though St. Paul says that if Christ be not risen our faith is vain (1 Cor. 15:14), he clearly teaches that it is Calvary which effected the salvation-redemption of the human race, *for by it our sins are forgiven*. Every school child knows of the saving significance of the cross of Christ and can repeat the story of the passion. The cross of Christ is a scandal and an enigma to Jew and Christian alike (Gal. 5:11; Cor. 17:24; Col. 2:14); yet Christians believe it is through the shedding of the innocent blood of Jesus that we have been redeemed and our sins forgiven (Eph. 1:7). Indeed, there can be no forgiveness of sin without the shedding of blood (Heb. 9:15-22), not the ineffective blood of goats and heifers (Heb. 9:11-12), but the blood of a special

Paschal Victim given to us by the Father himself (1 Cor. 5:7). Though he was sinless, the Father made Jesus into sin for us, so that in him we might be turned into the holiness of God (2 Cor. 5:21). For our sake, Jesus freely chose to be burdened with the curse invoked by the Law against all transgressors (Gal. 3:13). It is the Father who has sent his Son and has willed his sacrifice, for he did not spare his own Son but gave him up for us to death as a victim for our sins (Rom 3:24).

When that oft-repeated account is given in the words of Scripture, it tends to be simply accepted by Christians because it sounds so authentic and authoritative. Its difficulties are overlooked. I am indebted, therefore, to the late Walter Imbiorski for the following contemporary account which highlights one of the more serious drawbacks by caricaturing it. (*An Address to Students*—Institute of Pastoral Studies, Loyola University, July 1973.)

You see, part of our difficulty is that most of us are caught up emotionally in what I would call Anselmian Salvation Theology, which goes something like this. God created the world. Adam and Eve sinned. God got pretty damn sore, goes into a 10,000 year pout, slams the gates of heaven and throws the scoundrels out. So he's up there pouting and about 5,000 years go by and the Son comes up and gives him the elbow and says: "Hey Dad, now is the time to forgive those people down there." God says, "No. I don't like them, they offended my divine majestry, they stay out. Let's make another galaxy instead!" Five thousand more years go by and the Son comes up and says: "Aw come on, Dad, let's forgive them! Look, I tell you what I'm going to do. If you will love them again, I'll go down there and become one of them, then you'll *have* to love them because I'll be one of them." God looks at the Son and says: "Don't bank on it. That doesn't turn me on too much at all." So the Son replies, "All right, God-Father, I'll tell you what I'm going to do. I'll raise the ante. I'll make you an offer you *can't* refuse! I'll not only go down there and become one of them, I'll *suffer* for them, real blood—you know how that turns you on, Dad! How about it?" And God says: "Now you're talking. But it's got to be real torture and real blood—no God-tricks you understand. You've got to really *suffer*. And if you'll do that then I'll forgive them. But if they stray off the straight and narrow just that much—ZAP—I'm going to send them to hell so fast their heads will swim." *And that is what we have been calling the "good news" of the Gospel.*

Imbiorski merely makes explicit what is implied in the standard account and in the usual Christian understanding of salvation. That fact alone should convince us that something is not quite right. It is the Father, after all, who determines what will or will not "open the gates of heaven" or be salvific for us, which means that *he* freely chose to hold out for the blood offering of his own son. To say that he did so "out of love," either for us or for his son, merely adds to the confusion.

The account that we are redeemed by the death on the cross not only seems to indict the Father of a certain blood-lust; it also portrays him as himself contradicting what he had consistently told Israel, there was to be no human sacrifice. Indeed, the story of Abraham and Isaac was told to make that very point. After all was said and done, God did *not* allow Abraham to kill his son. Having revealed to Israel that human sacrifices were both ineffective and forbidden, is it really conceivable that the Father would agree to re-establish friendly relations with our race only on the condition of such an offering? Hardly. That would also be totally incompatible with the picture of the Father we have been given in the Prodigal Son story (Luke 15:11-32).

As a matter of fact, Christians have not always viewed the bloody death of Jesus on the cross as *the* saving act. Scripture scholars have identified three different early understandings of the significance of the death on the cross that preceded and influenced the New Testament accounts. If we recall that the Gospels were written down between the years 70 and 100 A.D., we have almost a half century between the time of the crucifixion and the New Testament documents. During that period, Christians interpreted the meaning of that death in a variety of ways.

Some who were familiar with the history and traditions of Israel saw the death of Jesus as the culmination of the prophetic tradition. This account of the crucifixion finds its way into the New Testament especially in the writings of Luke. (13:31-33; Acts 2:22-24, 5:30-31, 10:40). Jesus follows in a long line of prophets sent by God, but Israel rejects their message and murders them. In this account the death of Jesus is seen as a certain sign that he is an authentic prophet. He received the treatment that Israel meted out to so many of its prophets, rejecting them as false and taking their lives for having blasphemed by their false prophecy. But the Father vindicated Jesus by raising him from the dead, thus confirming him as the latter-day prophet of Israel.

It should be noted in this understanding of things that willful and sinful people, unwilling to change their hearts and accept the Reign of God, are the cause of the murder of Jesus. By raising Jesus from the dead, the Father not only validates the truth of Jesus' message, but also reveals that he is still present to Israel and that salvation, the forgiveness of sins, is therefore still possible. Salvation comes, as it always has, from the Yahweh-God, the Father of Jesus.

A second ancient tradition among the earliest Christians sees the death of Jesus as in accord with the divine plan for all of humankind: the only way to glory is through suffering. That is true not only for Jesus, but for each one of us. For the Christians in this tradition there was nothing particularly special about the fact that Jesus, who was completely innocent, suffered and died for righteousness. "It *had* to be that way." That is how God works in the world; all of humankind experiences that, and so it is fitting that the Son of Man should undergo the same experience. (See Mark 8:31, 9:12; Luke 17:25.) We who come after him are challenged by his life and death to accept and endorse the path of suffering he trod, and are given a unique model of how to cope with the inevitable suffering that leads to glory.

And as might have been expected, in an age when Christianity was still so close to its Jewish roots, there was a third tradition which viewed the death of Jesus as a sacrificial expiation of human sins, reconciling and redeeming the human race. It was this third account of the death of Jesus that came to be the normative one and that raises such problems in contemporary, non-Hebrew minds. If, as we have just seen, Christians have not always understood that we are saved by means of the crucifixion, are those early Christians disqualified from being authentically Christian for that reason? If not, then perhaps neither are we.

It is instructive to note that each of these ancient accounts of the crucifixion arose from Jewish roots, but only one of them is open to an exclusively juridical and legalistic interpretation, the third one. If, as we have claimed, faith and religion were inextricably mixed throughout the Old Testament and also in the lives of the early Christians, it should not surprise us that the juridical account came to the fore and practically excluded all other interpretations of the crucifixion, and so became central to the New Testament.

According to Joseph Fitzmyer, S.J., the Scripture writers were well aware of the wide variety of perspectives available to them in interpreting the meaning of the crucifixion. They chose to use many different "metaphors" to proclaim their faith, and it was the more legalistic and literalistic patristic and scholastic thinkers who took the expiation "metaphor" literally and drove all other accounts from the scene. Fitzmyer expressly exonerates St. Paul on this point, claiming that a thorough study of his writings shows that he interpreted the crucifixion from several different points of view and not just one. (See *Jerome Biblical Commentary*, 79:81-97.) This corroborates Imbiorski's claim that the usual account of salvation is really part of Anselmian Salvation Theology. It was St. Anselm (1033-1109) who presented a finely honed account of why Jesus became human and had to die to save us. His *Cur Deus Homo* is a masterpiece and became the classical theological doctrine regarding redemption, punishment, satisfaction, etc. Scripture allows us much more freedom in interpreting the significance of Jesus' passion and death.

The usual Christian understanding of how our salvation was effected not only casts aspersions on the Father, it equally defames Jesus as well. Jesus spent his public life preaching the Good News of the Reign of God, and it can be assumed that the deepest desire of his heart was that people would respond to his proclamation and have a change of heart. But if he knew that the human race could only be saved on the condition of his own bloody murder, then he could not want "everyone" to be transformed by his message. If "everyone" responded to the Good News, there would be none left to administer his violent death. To hold that it was only through his passion and death on the cross that we were saved amounts to nothing less than saying that Jesus was a hypocrite about his preaching. It is far more likely that he really did hope and pray that "everyone" would respond to his call, and that the significance of his death must be otherwise.

Regarding the death of Jesus, two distinct questions must be asked: Why did he die? Why did he die as he did? The answer to the first question is disarmingly simple. *Jesus died because he was human.* Scripture assures us that he was like us in all things save sin (Heb. 4:15), but there is only one way out of this world once you are born of woman: you must die. Jesus, though the incarnate Son of God, was not exempt from this basic law of human life. By the very act of choosing to become human, he was also choosing to die one day. Incarnation involves dying. To say otherwise would be to deny that Jesus was fully human.

Destined to die just because he was human, Jesus was not, however, predestined to die in one way rather than another. We have failed to understand that the Old Testament prophecies need only give testimony to the fact that Jesus died as he did; *they in no way make it necessary that he die that way.* Those who hold that it is by his death on the cross that Jesus redeemed the world must ask themselves a pointed question: Would anything have been different had Jesus died in some other way? Suppose that the Jews had heard his call and the nation was converted. Suppose further that he therefore went out beyond Israel preaching the Good News of the Coming Kingdom. And, finally, suppose that while on one of those ''missionary'' journeys he sustained a fatal accident. Would that have made any difference in the salvific effect of his life and death? If so, what? Or suppose he lived to be 98 years old, remaining faithful to the dream to the end, and finally succumbed to old age, totally spent and exhausted by his labors. What then?

Are we really ready to say that for the Son to have become human, to have lived and walked among us, to have preached the Reign of God and then incarnated it personally for all to see—are we really ready to say that all of that would go for naught and be of no salvific value? Why must Jesus be *murdered* in order to save us? The only possible answer is that the Father willed it that way. But we have already seen that that answer is not without difficulties of its own. Why won't we admit that it is not crucifixion which is redemptive but incarnation? Why do we insist on holding on to the most ''religious'' interpretation of the passion and death of Jesus when it presents such problems both to our experience and to our faith? Admittedly, salvation by crucifixion and immolation is one way to tell the story of our salvation. *It is the thesis of this book that it is neither the best nor the only way to do so.*

What should we say ''in faith'' about the passion and death of Jesus? What is the significance of the fact that in reality Jesus suffered a violent death and was murdered after all? Come to proclaim the Reign of God, Jesus also incarnated it for all to see. This won for him the animosity and undying opposition of those who had a vested interest in keeping their world as it was, those who wanted no part in *metanoia,* repentance, transformation, or divinization. Their ways were not God's ways. They failed to heed the wise counsel of people like Gamaliel and so ultimately ending up ''fighting God''—literally. They determined to be rid of Jesus, and crucifixion was the best available means at their disposal for doing that, given the historical realities of the time. The murder of Jesus was exclusively and fully willed by his enemies, not by him or the Father.

What are we to make of the fact that Jesus gave up his life freely? Must we charge him with complicity in his own murder? Of course not. Even in accepting death at the hands of his enemies, Jesus was incarnating the very Reign of God he proclaimed. The crucifixion is the most dramatic evidence we have of how far Love is willing to go for us, and as such it is central to our faith, but we are not obliged to see the cause of our salvation in that singular event.

Jesus as Savior/Redeemer

As we get more and more in touch with our Jewish roots, we may be able to gain a clearer perspective on the whole redemptive process. For the Adam and Eve I in each of us, God is everywhere evident in his works which proclaim his power and glory. He is everywhere, but at the same time above and beyond everything. *This irony makes intimacy with God impossible for Adam and Eve I.* For when they turn to face (confront?) the Master of Creation whose presence is everywhere evident, he is suddenly remote and enveloped in mystery. The Transcendent God of the Cosmos overwhelms us, fills us with an awe bordering on fear. We feel ourselves to be very small in his presence and very much alone.

For the Adam and Eve II in us, this cosmic existential loneliness is unbearable. We long to meet our God on a personal level, *where we can be near him and yet still feel free in his presence.* We hunger for an intimacy in which the God who is hidden reveals himself to us. Through faith we know that the miracle of revelation actually did occur in Jesus of Nazareth, who *is* the incarnate revelation of the Father. What we may perhaps not have understood is that the miracle of revelation in which the God-who-is-hidden reveals himself is one and the same miracle whereby we humans shed our masks and become revealed.

Put another way, Adam and Eve II's desire to really encounter their God is just the other side of their desire to reveal their deepest selves in intimacy. Who has not experienced at some time in her life a deep longing to have done with masks and subterfuges, lies and hypocrises, and all the games of power, manipulation, and abuse we play with one another? All of which is to ask, who among us has not felt a profound need for salvation/redemption? It is clear that only the presence of God to humankind can answer that need. It is intimacy, or if you prefer "incarnation," which redeems. *Jesus is our Savior/Redeemer because he is the complete embodiment of the absolute intimacy of God and all of humanity.* We are ourselves redeemed to the degree that we become like him.

Jesus, as the incarnate togetherness of God and human nature, guarantees in his person that intimacy with God is possible for us. In fact, he *is* the revelation that it is the Father's fondest desire to enter into a relationship of intimacy with each of us. It was through the Covenant that the Yahweh-God, the Father, freely entered into the society of human persons, thus making community possible. And as was true of all Jewish covenants, and is true of all human groupings which are authentic communities, the parties to them "encounter" one another in *freedom, reciprocity,* and *equality.* Jesus is the living incarnation of that redeeming truth of faith.

But that's precisely the problem. Human beings are wary of relating to God in freedom, reciprocity, and equality. That strikes us as an intolerable human arrogance. What good to us is a

God who "encounters" us in redemptive intimacy? What good is a God who does not command? What good is a God who has eschewed transcedence for intimacy? What good is the God of Adam and Eve II who does not come on out of power and might? The Adam and Eve I in us finds such a God of no earthly use, and so prefers in his stead a more "religious" sort of God, a God we can call on to bring down thunder and lightning in our enemies, a powerful God in whose presence we can feel small and insignificant, but protected and safe. The only trouble is that is not how Yahweh and Jesus have revealed themselves to us. Jesus did not come in order to do great things for people. Many tried to get him to do things for them, and he always responded graciously, but that was *not* his main ministry. To the consternation of many, he seemed content simply to be *present*, to be truly "with them." They may have wanted him to *do* more, but if they were open to it, it was his *presence* that transformed and divinized them.

The essence of Christianity lies in "incarnation," for Yahweh is the God-with-all-his-people; and Jesus, his Son and our Lord, is Emmanuel, which is to say, "God-with-us." The fundamental trait of their relations with humankind is their *redemptive presence*. The coming of the Lord shows the Father's fidelity to his original promise of intimacy with us. The Church, the New Israel, breaks with its most ancient faith-traditions when it settles for anything less, as it so often does. It can never settle for a grudging obedience or a heartless and perfunctory performance of rites. The call to walk with the Lord is fundamentally a call to *intimacy*. Anything less frustrates both people and the God of faith.

CHAPTER EIGHT

Walk With the Lord

At the beginning of his monumental work, *The Denial of Death,* Ernest Becker puts his finger on a central truth of human life. We live in a world of symbols and dreams. His exact words are:

> Man is not just a blind glob of idling protoplasm, but a creature who lives in a world of symbols and dreams and not merely matter. His sense of self-worth is constituted symbolically. He is a symbolic self, a creature with a name and a life history.

As I understand him, Becker means to say more than that each of us is a mysterious blend of the organic and symbolic. He is affirming that *to a human person nothing is merely as it appears.* For behind all the appearances of things, we strain to discover their meaning and significance for us. This is graphically demonstrated to us by our children. We casually distribute the cookies for dessert, only to be met with the complaint: "She got a bigger cookie than I did!" Or we jump in the car to take the kids to the beach only to have the joyful expectation dampened with: "But he sat up front the last time." The things we do with and for our children are not just things we do; they are the precious symbols that convey to them how we feel about them.

To give one a bigger cookie, or to allow another to sit up front more often is to send the message that we love and care for one more than another. At least this is how siblings view the matter. But when you come right down to it, in the game of life we're all siblings. How else explain that in our relations with others everything they say or do is interpreted symbolically by us as a measure of our own self-worth? And if the message we pick up does not coincide with the view we have of ourselves, we experience great pain.

Faced with pain, we humans usually adopt one of two basic strategies. Either we attack the source of the pain in an aggressive maneuver of some sort or failing that, we withdraw in sullen silence and seek out others in whose presence our self-worth is affirmed. The results in either case are the same. Intimacy, for which we desperately yearn and without which we cannot be fully human, is shattered.

Assuming that we can agree that this is a reasonably accurate account of the human condition, and that each of us can easily recognize herself in it, what are we to make of all this? Some would say that this is merely a recognizable vestige of our evolutionary journey from the sub-human, self-preservation, and the survival of the fittest. Undoubtedly, that is how it *appears*. But, if Becker is right, then as symbolic beings we must strive to get behind the appearances of our world and we shall find no peace until we do.

That in itself is very illuminating. *It would make absolutely no sense at all for people to be symbolic if things were as they seem.* But if human life is not what it seems, there are only two alternatives: Human life is either *absurd* or it is *ironic*.

As Christians we are prevented from taking the first alternative seriously, but for persons without faith the second alternative is equally unacceptable. Thus humankind is divided into three main classes: 1) those who take life as it comes accepting it for what it is worth on the surface; 2) those who are either convinced or have a strong hunch that there is more to life than meets the eye; 3) those who can't quite make up their minds and so vacillate, as the occasions demand, between the other two. Judging from the way life is going these days, it would seem that the numbers of those who take life as it appears is on the increase. More and more people appear willing to live in a world without *irony* or *intimacy,* which means more and more people are accepting the dehumanization which everywhere abounds. But to accept that situation is not a passive act; to accept dehumanization is to further it, to increase its strength and power.

What appears on the surface as a move toward dehumanization, reveals itself on deeper inspection and in the light of faith as *sin*. The real power of sin is not that it enslaves and crushes individual sinners, which it does, but that it becomes established in a culture, gains a reputation, is accepted as the taken-for-granted way of doing things and, in short, becomes a living tradition. Like all traditions, the tradition of sin embodies a definite value system and gives human life a recognizable direction, i.e., *inward, backward,* and *deathward.* (See John Shea, *What A Modern Catholic Believes About Sin,* Thomas More, 1971.)

Sin moves *inward,* that is to say, away from the intimacy to which Yahweh Elohim called Adam and Eve II. Sin moves *backward,* that is to say, away from the Coming of the Kingdom which the Lord Jesus heralded and toward which he pointed. And sin moves *deathward,* that is to say, away from the creative newness of life with which we are all graced in the Spirit and which was confirmed by the risen Lord. Left to itself, our world seems to move irrevocably in a sinful direction.

But in faith we all know that our world has not been left alone. Unable to bear the inward, backward, and deathward drift of human life, and yet unwilling to confront us or force us into a lifeward direction, because such an act would make intimacy with him forever impossible, the Lord God chose to show us the way by becoming even more intimate with us. He entered our history and became one of us. He does not, however, break down the door of our hearts. There is never any force or coercion, just the ever continuing *invitation to intimacy.* On the surface we appear to be stubborn and unwilling to "yield," but ironically God knows of the Adam and Eve II at our center. He is consistent in his calling us as he waits patiently for us to respond.

While on the earth, the Lord never preached fire and brimstone; that was the invention of the more humorless of his followers in every age who have no taste either for irony or intimacy. No, he preferred to challenge us by invitations clothed in irony, which we call parables. A parable appears to be a story about somebody else. In truth, it is aimed at surprising the hearer with a personal experience of God's present and intimately personal call. Parables are not objective doctrinal statements so much as vocational summonses calling the hearer to participate in faith in the reality which Jesus is. Teaching, even the most non-directive, attempts to at least persuade if not to force assent, but parables are much more respectful of human freedom. Jesus simply speaks the parable; it is up to us to decide. The real power of a parable is its ability to reveal to us in a flash what we normally keep well hidden from consciousness, i.e., the deeper dimensions of our lives and their future possibilities. The self-righteous and comfortable think the parables are for somebody else, and so miss the point of it all. Others hear the divine call contained in the parable, but are afraid to risk the intimacy of response. Those who hear the parables and take them to heart, walk with the Lord and become *signs* of the Kingdom. (See John Shea, *The Challenge of Jesus*, Thomas More, 1975, esp. Ch. 2 "Jesus As Challenge," also available from Doubleday [Image Books] 1977.)

But if a parable is an ironic invitation to intimacy, an invitation that challenges the hearer and invites him to risk his surface life to gain authentic life more deeply, then we are justified in calling Jesus himself "The Parable of God." For he is the enfleshed invitation of God. While respecting our freedom, he challenges the everydayness of our daily lives and calls us to be our truer selves in intimacy with him. And so unrelentingly down through the ages we hear the gentle invitation: "Come, walk with me!"

Those who try to respond generously to the "Parable of God" soon realize that membership in the Christian community commits them to struggle to give human life the direction Jesus gave it—that is *outward, forward,* and *toward resurrection.* As Church, we form a counter-culture to our world, but a counter-culture of a most ironic sort. We seek not to coerce and badger our neighbors, but to live our lives of intimacy in trusting openness to them, always hoping that they may see in us something of the "parable of God," and finally get the point of it all. That is what it means for us to be a *sign-community.*

Yet we bear the heavy burden of knowing that despite our best intentions we have not ourselves always responded fully to the trust the Lord places in us. We recognize, all too well, the inward, backward, and deathward power of sin in our lives. Often we feel like hypocrites and are tempted to join our world in its admission that humankind is unsuited to "walk with the Lord." But we must resist that temptation because in our heart of hearts we know it is not true. To that end, we should gather frequently with men and women of faith whom we admire, to feel the power of their faith, and to somehow find the strength to risk intimacy despite our inadequacies.

Like the apostle Thomas who found it hard to go on believing without touching the Lord, we should, in our struggle to be faithful, gather with believers from time to time and touch the Lord anew in one another and in our retelling of the story of Jesus. Not, by any means, the story of the historical Christ, but of the ironic Jesus who not only was not quite what he appeared to be, but who assured us that we aren't either. Of course, in retelling the story of Jesus, we are in some way telling the story of each one of us who has chosen to walk with him.

What Say We of Jesus?

Jesus looked the son of Joseph the carpenter. He dressed like any other Nazarene, and when in the big city was obviously recognized as something of a country bumpkin. And for some, that was all they ever saw in him. But there were others, not many, who sensed something marvelous about him. They noticed that whenever they were in his presence they felf freer than they had ever felf before. After encountering him, they found it hard to stay centered on themselves, their cares and concerns, as their attention began to shift noticeably outward toward others. They began to "see" and "hear" things that had escaped them before. Most marvelous of all, they found that they no longer lived in fear. No one was quite sure why all these wonderful things were happening, but they all agreed that it was great just being near him.

After awhile, some began to catch on a little, not much, but a little. Life away from him began to be seen as not-life. And so a handful of people decided to risk everything, which ironically they now saw as nothing, to walk with him. For three years they were inseparable, during which time it finally dawned on some of them that this Jesus fellow was truly a man of God. They began to understand that all the wonderful things that had occurred were due to the *presence of God*. That was it! God's hand was at work in their midst. And as we have seen in *Our Story* (6), one day, toward the end, in a fit of enthusiasm, Philip, asked Jesus when he would reveal the Father to them. At that moment, the truth about Jesus of Nazareth was revealed to us. ''I and the Father are one,'' he said.

We have interpreted that to mean that Jesus *is* God. And so he is. But there is another, more ironic truth contained there, the appreciation of which Christians are only coming to slowly. Jesus was revealing not only who *he* was, but also who *we* are—at least in our noblest parts. For what Jesus was saying to Philip was that the divine is not to be found outside of humankind but within, in the intimacy and togetherness of God and human beings, promised and foretold in the Covenant, effected and realized in the Lord Jesus, and present in each one of us when we truly walk with him in faith.

This revelation is literally unbelievable; it is simply too ironic. After all, it is far easier to think of intimacy with God solely in terms of our relating to *him*. Redemptive intimacy becomes so much more difficult for us if God has been so indiscreet as to have identified himself with all of humankind. *It would mean that the route to divine intimacy runs through the whole human race!* Precisely. That is the very heart of the Christian faith, and Jesus leads the way. Jesus *is* the Way, and all are invited to join the parade and fall in alongside him.

But how can I tell if I am really ''walking with the Lord''? Easily enough. To walk with the Lord is to have the very same effect on people that he did. After encountering us, do people feel freer, fear less, walk taller, think nobler, sing more joyfully, and feel more alive than ever before? Do we present an enhancing presence to our world? Or are we, in our relations with others, like caricaturists who feel compelled to exaggerate their every fault and magnify their every flaw? Do we achieve our self-worth at the expense of others (à la Adam and Eve I), feeling whole ourselves only if we can demonstrate the fragmentation in others? If so, then we have dropped out of the parade. When we so act we show ourselves to be men and women of little faith. We no longer believe in the Covenant of intimacy; we no longer believe in the alternate lifestyle offered to the world by Jesus; we no longer believe in the greatness of our fellow human beings, and we have stopped believing in our truest selves. The loss of *intimacy* always begins with our inability to ''see'' the Lord, one another, and ourselves with sufficient *irony*.

Really Acting Like Adam and Eve II

The great Christians of every age and those of our day like John XXIII, Martin Luther King, Jr., and Mother Teresa of Calcutta give powerful witness to this truth. They are able to love so completely precisely because they do not "see" things the way the rest of us do. Why is that so? Perhaps one could say they have more "faith" than the rest of us, but that explains nothing because it merely repeats that they "see" things differently than we do. Or it could be that they are more generous than we are. But that doesn't get us very far either, since we all agree on that and are seeking a reason *why* they are more generous.

Each of those remarkable persons began just as you and I did. Each of them was judged ordinary by their fellows for a good portion of their lives. But then suddenly they stood out as being wonderfully different. In each case, one could point to a moment when they seemed to come more alive, to be reborn, and to "walk with the Lord" in new and unmistakable ways. What happened?

There is no certainty in such matters, but I would like to attempt an explanation. As human beings each of us acts often enough out of our needs and compulsions. We become compulsive doers of whatever it is we are doing. We become compulsive workers, compulsive players, compulsive love-makers, and at times we have been known to even practice our "religion" compulsively. But actions done out of need or compulsion are propelled, as it were from the agent and go banging headlong into the world. They "confront" and even "affront" whatever and whomever they meet. Such a mode of action is quite effective in the world of things, and is perhaps the best way to get things done. The trouble is that there is also a world of persons out there who are "done in" in the process. One can hardly imagine the Lord acting that way.

Fortunately, we do not *always* act out of need or compulsion. There are times, very special times (Time II), when we act out of our own charism or gift. At first we are not aware that this is what we are doing. Initially, we only notice that sometimes when we act we affect others in much the same way as the Lord did, and that when we so act we become a beneficent and enhancing presence for them. We are a bit embarrassed by the fact that their just seeing us, across a room or down the street, is enough to bring a smile to their faces. They are happier just knowing we are there. But like the apostles, we begin after awhile to realize something, namely, that at those times, we are acting out of our special gifts. We would never have been able to discern this by ourselves; we learn of our gifts from others. Conversely, they learn of their gifts from us. For in our smiles, loving glances, joyful songs, and feelings of enhancement is revealed to them their truest and most gracious selves.

What I am suggesting is this: were it not for the experiences of gracing and being graced, we should never develop the skill to see life, in ourselves and in others, ironically. We would miss the "gift dimension" of life without which genuine intimacy is little more than an idle hope. Since we are not born with the ability to see life ironically, it must come to us later in life. And so it does, for our ability to see deeply enough to discover our own gifts and to discern the gifts in others is undoubtedly the most precious gift we receive from our intimacy with others. Until we have had our eyes opened to this central mystery of life, we are not really able to "walk with the Lord." The fact is we don't even know there is a parade and celebration going on.

I suspect that it was only after their true gifts were revealed to them by others that John XXIII, Martin Luther King, Jr., and Mother Teresa of Calcutta began to see ironically enough to allow them to desire to construct a life around their charisms and gifts rather than around their needs and compulsions. They began to feel a tremendous solidarity between themselves, the Lord, and all the rest of humankind. The divisions that lie on the surface of life began to melt, and they began to see clearly the truth of Jesus: *God and human beings are irrevocably together*. And once all that happened, it was only a matter of time before they moved to the forefront of the parade of those who "walk with the Lord."

How good it is to go over the story of Jesus with true believers! But as I have already suggested, the story of Jesus is really the story of each one of us. For we all have been touched by people who have not only graced us by putting us in touch with our own gifts, but have graciously lavished themselves on us as well. Small wonder that we are so happy when we are with those people. For it is when we are with them that we have renewed hope that the Kingdom really is coming, that intimacy really is possible, and though the road leads to Calvary we need not be afraid. Our compulsions would make us fearful and urge us to run. But if we have learned anything from one another, it is that we are not to be afraid. We are his people and we hear his loving voice: "Do not be afraid, for I am with you. I have called you by your name, and you are mine." *As his people, we have come to know and understand the central mystery of life–divine graciousness and intimacy.*

Our task as Christians, right to the end, is to witness to that truth. We must continue to grace our world with our lives in the hope that the world will soon come to realize its own great gifts. To turn back is unthinkable for us. Yet we do grow weary on the way. We do lose our ironic sense and start to believe that things are as they appear. At such times it helps to celebrate a little, to celebrate the intimacy we have experienced, to celebrate what we have been, what we are, and what we can become together as we continue to walk with the Lord.

CHAPTER NINE

Know Me

I am sure it is not difficult to detect some of the pain and passion behind my account of redemptive intimacy. From childhood on, we have been cautioned not to take the name of the Lord in vain (Ex. 20:7). The "religious" version of how God works in the world seems to me to do just that. Much of what "religious" Christians say about God amounts to slander against the Father. I have asked myself how such misunderstandings could ever have happened, and once they occurred, how they could have been blindly protected from criticism and then handed down as Good News. This is all the more mystifying when one reflects on the fact that life and our lived experience constantly and consistently witness otherwise. Must we say, with Kierkegaard, that "it is not until evening comes and days decline that one understands . . ."? Perhaps he is right; after all, I did not come to my current understanding until I was well along in life.

Still, I am reluctant to say that it is wrong-headed for us to attempt to share that faith perspective with the young, because they cannot possibly understand. If God dwells in humankind, then experience is revelatory and one can come to *really know him* at any stage of life. Many of the young know the truth but are reluctant to speak out because so many of their more experienced elders do nothing to encourage them, so wedded are they to the religious version of Christianity.

Yet, as *Our Story* suggests, in every age there is always a remnant, of old and young alike, who have deciphered the irony of life and who know and live the truth, thus keeping the dream alive. The resurgence of fundamentalism has put today's "remnant" under ever-increasing pressure. It seems inevitable that the final decades of the twentieth century will witness a sharpening of this conflict within the Church. In the midst of the ensuing turmoil, the operative question, as it has always been in such situations, is who most truly "knows" the Father. So this final chapter is devoted to that question.

To put the matter in perspective, the following scriptural montage might be helpful.

Hear the word of the Lord, O people, for the Lord has a grievance against the inhabitants of the land: There is no fidelity, no mercy, *no knowledge of God in the land.*

My people are fools—*they know me not.* They are senseless children having no understanding of me, but they are wise in evil, knowing not how to do good. It is love I desire, not sacrifices, and *knowledge of God,* not holocausts. I will give them a heart with which to understand I am the Lord. They shall yet be my people and I will be their God, for they shall return to me with their whole heart.

Proclaim the greatness of God, a faithful God without deceit. Yet he has been treated basely by his children. Is the Lord to be thus repaid by us? Is he not our Father who created us? Has he not made us and established us? In this struggle to know the Father, our weapons are not merely human. They possess God's own power for the destruction of all sophistries, and every proud pretension which is raised up against *authentic knowledge of God.* For we know the Son of God has come and has given us discernment to recognize the One who is true. And we ourselves are in the One who is true, for we are in his Son, Jesus Christ. For the Lord himself prayed:

Father, the hour has come! Give glory to your Son that your Son may give glory to you, inasmuch as you have given him authority over all humankind that he may bestow eternal life on those you gave him. And eternal life is this: *to know you,* the only true God.

And so we pray unceasingly, asking that we may attain full knowledge of him through perfect wisdom and spiritual insight. Then we shall lead lives worthy of the Lord and pleasing to him in every way. We will multiply our good works and *grow in the knowledge of God.*

(Hosea 4:4; Jer. 4:22; Hosea 6:6-7; Jer. 24:7; Deut. 32:3-6; 2 Cor. 10:5; John 17:2-3; Col. 1:9-10.)

Do We Really Know Him?

Without doubt, the strongest impression one takes from this collage is that the one single thing asked of us is that we *know him*. It is the one absolutely necessary and indispensable thing not only for Christians but for anyone who wants to respond to the presence of God in life. We find that difficult to accept, first because we think we already do know him and second, because we think that there are other things equally or more important.

With regard to the first, it is possible for us to think that because we are Christians and have read the Bible and have mastered the trick of knowing how to talk about God, i.e., of using words correctly in a religious and theological way, that we *know God*. Nothing could be further from the truth. It does us little good to master a theological language when we have nothing to say in that language, when we have no "experience" of God in our lives. We cannot say the right things about God unless we have had a God-experience. Not the God-experience characteristic of Adam and Eve I, but rather the God-experience of Adam and Eve II. They knew that authentic knowledge of God cannot be achieved by our best efforts but must be allowed to "happen to us"; it can only be accepted as "gift."

As Gregory Baum observes: "Some things precious to man can be produced by will power or merited by personal effort, by *the important thing just happen to a man*. The profound things in human life are always gifts" (*Man Becoming,* Herder, 1970, p. 128). This is obviously true of intimacy, love, and friendship but it is also true of freedom, so precious to contemporary people. The freedom to enter into dialogue, to risk, to be intimate is not a power we have of ourselves, but is something we all experience as a gift from others. Why would it be otherwise with authentic knowledge of God?

Knowledge of God can "happen to us," but not if we demand it or try to attain it by human effort. It is the result of redemptive intimacy. Only when we cease our needless and empty questioning and striving and finally surrender to the Presence at our center do we catch a glimpse of the God of faith. Unmindful of that fact and impatient with that process, many refuse to wait in patience for authentic knowledge of God and, like the Jews of old who constructed a golden calf, construct a "religious" god of their own making. They then, quite correctly, claim to know him, as well they should, since they have manufactured every inch of him. Alan Watts in *Behold The Spirit,* (Random House, 1971) put it so very well:

> Man is always trying to manufacture God, or a sense of God for himself and therefore ignores the one that is actually given, because there is no credit to be gained in accepting a gift. Nevertheless, this truth is Gospel, Good News,—*we do not have to seek God* he is already here and now, and to seek for him implies that he is not. *There are a million methods for expressing knowledge and love of God, but not one for attaining it.* And yet the thing happens—God is known and God is loved.

If there is only one thing needful, i.e., knowledge of God, it should be noted that it must be "authentic" knowledge of God, not the human-made knowledge of a manufactured god. Only the former fully liberates and is truly redemptive. The latter is yet one more effect of the assertive Adam and Eve I in our lives. It is the *manufactured god of religion*

> who threatens us with thunder and lightning
> who visits his wrath on the children of Adam
> who is so insecure that he demands constant affirmation from
>   his creatures
> who forgives but does not forget
> who puts conditions on every spiritual gift
> who saves only Christians, viewing all others as infidels
> who wills human suffering and inflicts pain on humankind in
>   order to teach them a spiritual lesson
> who delights in the letter of the law
> who views women as second class members of the species
> who is satisfied if we but keep the commandments
> who sets up Church as an institutional intermediary between
>   himself and humankind
> who insists on marking the infinite chasm between the divine
>   and the human thus making real intimacy with him
>   impossible.

To know *that* God is not to know the Yahweh Elohim of Adam and Eve II, the Father of Jesus and the God who dwells within us; such knowledge is the very antithesis of the God of faith.

A second reason we may not think knowledge of God is uniquely central to the Christian enterprise is because we think that something else is. For example, loving God, praising God, keeping the commandments, living a good life, etc. Our scriptural montage made it clear that there are many other things that must make up the truly Christian life, but all of them are rooted in and are derived from authentic knowledge of God. For most of our lives we are, as Kierkegaard noted, "so busy" with other things (Time I) that we don't have time (Time II) to wait patiently for the voice of the God of intimacy to sound within us. If we could but still our assertive and achieving selves (Adam and Eve I) for a moment, we might be able to hear a voice which is generally inaudible amid the turmoils of contemporary American life:

> Stop all your rushing around. Stop all your striving. Be still. Be at peace. All I have ever asked of you is that you *know me*. For if you did but know me, you would be free to do good.

That, of course, is never easy, and especially not for hardheaded people with a "can do" spirit. But unless we quiet our restless spirits, "unself" ourselves enough to accept the gift of knowledge of God, we shall be forced to continue on under the mistaken religious assumption that we already know God. But do we?

Mechanisms of Unselfing

It sounds so simple—it sounds so inviting—it sounds so much more liberating than all the talk about rules, commandments, and obligations. All we have to do is *know him*. Why do we find it so hard? What is the chief obstacle that stands in the way of doing that? It is *ourselves*. Not, of course, our truest selves where justice and charity dwell, but the other part of us. Iris Murdoch in *The Sovereignty of Good* (Schocken Books, 1971) describes that other darker side:

> I assume that human beings are naturally selfish. This seems true on the evidence, whenever and wherever we look at them, in spite of a very small number of apparent exceptions. About the quality of this selfishness modern psychology has had something to tell us. The self, the place where we live, is a place of illusion, so *by*

opening our eyes we do not necessarily see what confronts us. The psyche is . . . relentlessly looking after itself. Its consciousness is not normally a transparent glass through which it views the world, but a cloud of more or less fantastic reverie designed to protect the psyche from pain. It constantly seeks consolation, either through imagined inflation of self or *through fictions of a theological nature.*

The central point in all of this is that the "self" so colors our perceptions that we can't quite be sure that what we know is reality; it may simply be reflections of the self. It is that same self which makes it hard for us to be sure we "know God" and not some theological fictions fashioned by our self for its own purposes. Unless we can find a way to "unself" ourselves, there is no hope that we will ever be in touch with reality or be able to know God as he calls us to.

The call of Yahweh-God, that the one important thing is that we know him, runs contrary to the natural inclinations of the self. The self is so busy with its own agenda; it protests that it does not have time to know him. The self's dearest desire is to have its own way, to manipulate and control life, others, and even the Yahweh-God. It refuses to learn the central lesson of life, *let it be.* The self pretends to see little value in knowing God, choosing instead religious practices based on theological fictions, because it senses that to really know him would require of it a radical change in both lifestyle and action.

Obviously, then, the first step to prepare for the "gift" of the knowledge of God is enough "unselfing" on our part to allow the revelation to happen in our lives. To that end, we must introduce *mechanisms of unselfing* into our lives. Such unselfing is the primary goal of any authentic spirituality. To recapture a lost spirituality is to reintroduce into our lives on a regular basis strategies for unselfing, so that we can "see" the invisible, "hear" the inaudible, "speak" the ineffable, and "know" the unknowable.

Coping With Failure

Nothing betrays us and reveals that we do not really know him more dramatically than the way we cope with failure. We Catholics are ill prepared to cope with failure because we have been overfed a theology of sin. We probably lack something desperately needed in our cruel and imperfect world, namely, a theology of failure. The Adam and Eve I in us will not face up to that easily. Lacking such a theology, we have generally made a botch of coping with birth control, divorce and remarriage, the transfers from priesthood and religious life, and the loss of our children to other Christian denominations, to other faiths, or to the new paganism. The air is filled with our self-righteous anger. Because we are so accustomed to identifying "failure" with "sin," *we don't know where to begin to give people permission to fail.* If we really knew him, we would stop trying to control and manipulate others for their own good, knowing full well that is not how God works in humankind.

This much is clear: we all fail. Because we are not perfect, because we were born with defects, we are in need of mending-healing in order to be whole and work well. Prior to such redemptive healing, we are going to make mistakes, wound others, betray friends, be unfaithful, reject gifts, and manipulate and deceive others to our own end. God knows this; only the Adam and Eve I in us makes us blind to it. If we did but know him, we'd also know ourselves. We'd know we have limits. We'd know ourselves as needy, and we'd give ourselves permission to fail. And once we had managed to do that, we might then find it possible to put aside our unrealistic expectations of others, permitting them to be, as we also are, *imperfect but loved by God.* We must learn to be gracious with ourselves and with others in the face of our and their failures to achieve our highest ideals. We must rid ourselves of the notion that being gracious in the face of failure is somehow to betray the ideal. Until we can do that, it is clear that we don't really know him.

It is only natural, I suppose, that a people who walk with the Lord and who commit themselves to his dream of the Coming Kingdom would find failure particularly troublesome. We Christians tend to see only the "risen Lord" and we forget the "struggling and failing Jesus." We are reluctant to admit that like us Jesus experienced failure. But the New Testament verifies not only that Jesus failed, but that the "Good News" he proclaimed and incarnated was directed primarily to those looked upon, then as now, as the moral and religious failures of the day.

During Jesus' Galilean ministry, whole towns rejected him, e.g., Chorazin, Bethsaida, and Capernaum (Luke 10:13; Matt. 11:20-24). So ineffective was his ministry in his home district that Scripture reminds us that no prophet is ever honored in his own country (Luke 4:24). Things got so bad that on one occasion, after people had walked away from him because they found his saying hard, Jesus asked his followers: "Will you also go away?" (John 6:67) In fact, it was this lack of success in his Galilean ministry that probably caused Jesus to decide to alter his strategy and "go up to Jerusalem," there to come face to face with his known enemies and to face the real possibility of ultimate rejection and death.

After a triumphal entry into Jerusalem, he looked down on the city one day and was moved to tears, saying "O Jerusalem, Jerusalem, you slay prophets and stone those who are sent to you! How often I have wanted to gather your children together as a mother bird collects her young under her wings, *but you refused me. If only you had known the path to peace this day,* but you have completely lost it from view" (Luke 13:35, 19:42). Finally, as if to underline the failure of his life project, while hanging on the cross, Jesus was taunted by the crowd: "If you are what you say, if you are not a failure, come down from the cross" (Matt. 27:40). And so it was he died, a sign of total rejection and failure.

If Jesus and his way of living were ultimately rejected by the majority, so also was his message. He proclaimed the Reign of God, the Reign of the Abba-God, of the God who is our Father. It was Jesus' Abba-experience that gave his message its distinctive meaning. It was that Abba-experience that gave Jesus true knowledge of God, something his contemporaries did not have. The heart of that experience and message is that *for everyone without exception* there is reason to hope. There are no conditions on that. *Redemptive intimacy is available to all.* The old religious image of a vindictive, mean, and jealous God was to give way to the God of faith, who cherishes people, all people, and has made his abode with them.

Jesus presented a God who does not demand but gives; does not oppress but raises up; does not wound but heals. A God who forgives instead of condemning, and liberates instead of punishing. *Woe, then, to those who demand, oppress, wound, condemn, and punish in his name! It can only be that they do not truly know him.* Throughout our long history, it has always been far too easy for us Christians to deceive ourselves into thinking that the Lord himself requires us to do such things. But then the parables of the Prodigal Son, the Good Shepherd, the Wedding Banquet, the Workers in the Vineyard, and the Wheat and the Weeds—all become major stumbling blocks and all but unintelligible to us.

It is not the Father, who made each of us, who named us in our mother's womb, and knows our rising up and our going down, who does these things. Whenever they occur, it is *we* who do them to one another. Such things stem from the fantasizing self, from our religious fictions, not from the Lord God who calls us to intimacy.

The Great "Amen"

Amid all the disputes among Scripture scholars about which sayings of Jesus are authentic, we can identify two words which undoubtedly were actually spoken by him. Both are "A" words, and they constitute the sum and substance of the experience of God, which Jesus wished to share with us. Those pivotal words are *Abba* and *Amen.* Or to put the matter in some sort of context: Because God is Father ("parent" if you are sensitive about sexist language), we are called to say and to live "Amen."

The signs that we have not fully learned the lesson of yielding and letting go, and cannot truly say Amen (Let It Be) are these: we are filled with anxiety over our failures and the failures of those we love; and because we are so troubled, we do not give off peace. We thus continue to look for new and more effective ways of our *doing something* about these situations. With the best intentions in the world, we begin to scheme, manipulate, and control the situation so that it comes out the way we think it should. We lack that characteristic that God reveals to those who really know him: patience.

If we consult our own experience and reflect on how God deals with each of us, we are well aware of him as a *present but waiting God.* He waits years for us to finally recognize his presence within ourselves. He gently calls us to greater and greater intimacy, remaining faithful to us; all the while we are toying endlessly with the idea of responding. He is in no hurry; he allows us the room and space we need. And when we finally turn to him, he, like the father in the Prodigal Son story, throws his arms around us in joy at our coming, effectively smothering our feeble apologies about why it took us so long. To say and live "Amen" is to give up pressuring either ourselves or others like the Abba-God who made us. In faith, we must *let ourselves and others be,* because we know that the Abba-God is at work in all of humankind. Our task is to stop meddling, and to live our own lives as witnesses and signs of that divine presence. It is that presence and the intimacy it offers which is redemptive, not our fearful badgering and threatening.

So, in truth, there is only one failure—ultimately: to turn from the light, to refuse to accept the revelation that the Abba-God makes of himself in each of us. It is to prefer a God of our own fashioning, one who puts more store in *doing* than in *being,* when we know in our hearts that we are called to say "Amen" to the redemptive presence of the Abba-God within.

If by the graciousness of the Abba-God, we have come to truly know him and to know how he operates in the world, then we are called to operate that way as well, and to proclaim that "Good News" to all who will listen, but most especially to our own loved ones. It may well happen that the institutional Church may proclaim a different God than the one who has revealed himself in our experience. Even so, according to what we have come to know about the Abba-God, we must say "Amen" to even that—*let it be.* But since *we also are Church,* we too must proclaim the God of faith as we have come to know him. (This is why I have undertaken to write this book.) We shall be unable to do that effectively unless we stop all our busyness from time to time, still our manipulative selves, and patiently wait for the awareness of him to happen in our lives.

This does *not* mean that we should be inactive, but it does mean that any action that flows from anything other than our knowing him can only add to the confusion in our lives. Once we know him, our actions will be truly godly and as St. Paul says: "We shall lead lives worthy of the Lord and pleasing to him in every way" (Col. 1:10).

Appendix

Building a Household Church:
A Theology of Base Communities

The difference between Christians who are evangelized and those who are not is the difference between *gospel-consumers* and *gospel-creators*. The *gospel-consumer* sees membership in the ecclesial community as an insurance policy for eternity of which she is the beneficiary. For the gospel-consumer, the Church is necessary because it has the Mass and the Sacraments which are the channels of the grace of salvation. Vatican II marked a change of direction for Catholics: they will henceforth be asked to give up this sort of self-centered religion, to cease being gospel-consumers, and to become gospel-creators.

The Christian who is a *gospel-creator* understands that the message of Christ is so revolutionary that it is almost inappropriate to call Christianity a religion. If religion distinguishes a sacred order of reality distinct from a profane daily life, if it holds out to its devotees a privileged path to salvation not available to outsiders, then Christianity is not only not a relition, it is an anti-religion.

The *gospel-creator* sees the ecclesial community as the divinely instituted sign of the Good News of the Coming of the Kingdom. This person sees membership in that community not as a privilege which insures her salvation, but rather an an opportunity to further the Lord's dream for the world. Since the world cannot believe what it cannot see, our only hope of convincing it of its true dignity and sacredness—and of the fact that no matter how bad things are going for the world at present the Lord promised that some day it would be the Kingdom—is by joining with others who share that dream, to live it now as a present sign of the reality which is to come. Small groups of Christians engaged in doing that are called *base communities*. Church is then not so much made up of the totality of gospel-consumers clustered geographically in parishes and dioceses, as of gospel-creators clustered in base communities, each of which is mounting the dream and announcing the Coming of the Kingdom.

The Parish and the Base Community

We have become accustomed to thinking of the parish as the basic unit of Church. That seemed obvious so long as the salvation of individual souls was taken to be the top priority of Church. The parish structure meets that priority splendidly, since it is a dispensary of saving grace right in the neighborhood where everyone can have ready access to it. But if the top priority of Church is to be a *sign* of the Coming of the Kingdom, then the parish is just too large and unwieldy to do that effectively. Thus in 1921, Max Weber in his *Sociology of Religion* made the astounding claim:

> Every significant impact which Christianity has made upon the social order in modern times has been built upon the pious lay conventicle, the small group of pious transformation, the small church within the Church, which strenuously combines religious socialization and the deepening in Christian self-identity with a steadfast insistence on worldly service and action.

And Louis Evely puts that same thought in more contemporary language in *If the Church Is to Survive* (Doubleday, 1972) pp. 16-17:

> The Gospel is not an ideology, but a life. It must be passed on by living men, by little groups sufficiently united in brotherhood for brotherhood to be communicated among them. The true Church is a community in which the Gospel of Jesus is lived. The faith is dying because so few of our contemporaries have ever gone beyond the Church-building and Church-administrating to the Church in which Christ is alive through the assembly of his members.

The parish cannot be the basic unit of Church because it is a *secondary community* whose major purpose is to offer programs and services and to gather large numbers in public acts of worship. Intimacy and faith-sharing cannot be the primary objective of a parish simply because there are too many people involved. The parish itself, then, is supposed to be built on *primary communities* where intimacy, interpersonal relations, and faith sharing can occur with regularity. A parish not based upon many different primary communities is a parish in trouble. Its people come together on Sunday, attend services, hear a short homily, and that is the end of it. Religious people and gospel-consumers may think that more than enough, but for people of faith and gospel-creators that is just not enough Christian formation to keep them alive in the Lord. They want, need, and have a right to more.

In a vital parish, people meet often during the month in ways that enliven their faith, keep them mindful of the dream, and motivate them to the kind of effort required to walk with the Lord these days. This may be a Bible study group, a prayer group, faith-sharing group, a liturgy group, etc. The importance of these kinds of basic communities cannot be overestimated, because Sunday liturgies are just not enough to keep the faith alive in us when our culture daily bombards us with values that contradict the Gospel and hinder the Coming of the Kingdom. A vital parish is really like a diocese. It is composed of many different base communities, and the pastor is really like a bishop, because he has not only his large congregation to shepherd, but a host of smaller groups which constitute that larger constituency.

One Kind of Base Community: The Dialogue Group

As practical North Americans, we tend to think that all groups should be action-oriented. People gather to do something together which they could not do alone. And as Christians we are aware of being called to service and ministry to others, in the name of the Lord. But such "doing" must flow from our "being." The life of Christian doing can only be sustained by faith and deep spirituality, and when people gather regularly for that purpose, we may call their group a "dialogue" or "faith-sharing" group.

Somehow we think we have to go around acting all the time, but the greatest human action of all is *dialogue in the name of the Lord*. Dialogue was the very dynamic which the Lord himself followed in building Church and announcing the Coming of the Kingdom. Day in and day out the Lord engaged in dialogue on the gut issues of what life is all about. He not only taught people, *he listened to them,* which means *he dialogued!* If Church is to be a sign of the Kingdom, then dialogue on life, on its meaning, and how to transform it is *the* essential Church work.

In most of our lives there are five or six areas where the tension occurs between the Lord's dream of the Kingdom and our culture's view of progress: sex, family, politics, education, business and economics, and Church. (Can you think of any others?) These are the areas where we usually find ourselves enslaved and in real need of liberation. It is to these areas that the Good News of the Gospel is especially addressed. But before running off to engage in action in these areas where the culture and the Gospel conflict, we must first spiritualize the conflict by giving an insight from faith into what sex, family, politics, education, business and economics, and Church really are.

(Many programs set up in parishes fail to interest or attract people because they don't address the areas in which the people feel themselves enslaved and in need of liberation and salvation. When you choose one of these areas of tension for your program, you find that people not only come, but they have a lot to say on the subject. To succeed, parish programs must be set up in the light of where the people of the parish are experiencing real pain.)

But to dialogue on these gut issues is not the same thing as having a discussion of them. In a discussion those with the most education, the most training, the coolest heads, or who have the most skill at being clever tend to dominate and override the others. There always seems to be a winner and losers. Dialogue is very different. In a dialogue each person's voice is respected and heard; time is available for each person to speak; there is no domination. Each participant in a ''dialogue'' shares from his or her own lived experiences. There is no winner, and there are no losers.

Since we believe that God is present in human experience, the sharing of experiences eventually illuminates what the Lord is trying to tell us in the experiences about which we dialogue. And when that dialogue on gut issues is joined to a prayerful consideration of Scripture, then the word of God with all its power and might to motivate and transform can be felt by the group. This does not happen at every meeting, but when it does happen, the dialogue group feels validated, and each member finds the strength and motivation needed to support his or her individual ministry or social action in the world.

Suggested Pastoral Principles
for Base Communities

1. Nothing happens unless there is first a dream! Carl Sandberg, one of America's great poets, said that. Accepting that for a moment, what is the dream of Christianity? For too many that dream goes no further than saving one's own soul. When the dream is presented in that way, it capitalizes on the natural self-interest in each of us. Self-interest is, after all, the engine of most of our actions. But because presenting Christianity that way is so self-centered, it hardly does justice to the Lord who was "the man for others." The dream of the Lord was that one day the world would *be* the Kingdom, and by incarnating that dream, he became someone who meant something to others. The goal of base communities is to help members share and mount a common dream, to help them incarnate that dream as a sign to others, just as the Lord did.

2. People only believe in "incarnation"! People don't believe in programs, dogmas, institutions, rules, or rituals; they only believe in "incarnation." Like the apostle Thomas, we seem to believe only in what we can see, feel, or experience. That is why so many believed in the Lord. He incarnated the great dream of the Kingdom in his very person. That is also why we in our own day believe in people like Pope John XXIII and Mother Teresa of Calcutta. The institutional Church can teach and preach, liturgize and threaten, but unless there is an identifiable group who lives the dream, people simply will not believe. A base community aims at becoming such a group. As the basic unit of Church, it aims at so incarnating that dream that people will have something to believe in other than Buick and Eastern Airlines.

3. The world believes in "God," but we Christians don't! The world thinks God is a supernatural being who sits on a throne somewhere "up there," looking down on us, watching us, testing us, punishing us if we are bad, and rewarding us if we are good. That's the God that *we don't believe in at all*. We believe in Yahweh, the Lord God of Israel, the God of Abraham and Moses, the Father of Jesus. With the coming of Christ we now know definitively where God is. He is not in religious images, laws, or rituals; he is not in Jerusalem, Mecca, or even Rome. He is *not* in some far-off heaven. No, he is where he has always been: with, among, and in his people, especially in our noblest parts where justice and charity dwell. The base community gathers in the certain knowledge that God dwells with them, and that if they are attentive to his voice, they can even hear his Word in their midst.

4. The Word of God forms and fashions a people! The Word of God, the most powerful force for change, for love, and for freedom is not to be found in the Scriptures alone, for they are only one element of the Word. The Word of God powerfully transforms the situation and makes all things new when the Scriptures are brought into contact with the lived experiences of the people in whom the Lord dwells. It is the Word of God that fashions the group into a formed people who are a sign of the Kingdom. The base community must meet around the Gospels and their own experiences of the Lord living within them. Only thus can we as a scriptural people remain faithful to our tradition.

5. All roads lead to Calvary! People who walk with the Lord and mount the dream of the Coming Kingdom should not expect to be received with graciousness by the world. Those who have a vested self-interest in keeping the Kingdom from coming usually strike out strongly against all prophetic voices and lives. The culture will invariably treat harshly those who are signs of the Kingdom. The base community knows this and is willing to walk with the Lord even though the road leads to Calvary. Calvary can be a frightening experience, especially if you must walk there alone. So walk in that direction together, arm in arm, singing and celebrating on the way, preferring to walk together with the Lord than to take the easy path that our culture offers.

Practical Suggestions for Dialogue and Faith-Sharing Groups

1. Meet "in the name of the Lord." People are hungry for faith sharing. Don't let the meeting deteriorate into a social event; another party is eminently dispensable. Socializing should follow the serious business of the gathering.

2. Don't let the group become too large—just enough to fit in a living room. Ten to fifteen people may be ideal.

3. It will be slow going at first. Be patient with one another and with the initial ineffectiveness of the group. There is no community without tears. And it usually takes more time than you think it should.

4. To begin, make a short-term commitment. Agree to meet for six times. After that, re-evaluate and see if there is a consensus that it is worth going on. Then agree to meet six more times and evaluate again. By

then you should know whether you want to make a longer commitment and whether the meetings are important to you. In any case, be faithful to your commitments. Don't quit just because you had one or two bad meetings.

5. As for format, there is no fixed or normative way to conduct your time together. It should be done in the name of the Lord. There should be some shared prayer, some processing of Scripture, and some dialoguing about gut issues. You will find or create the format that suits you best.

6. There can be no base community without a *Peter*—some person or several who take the enterprise so seriously that they take on the vocation of being the "rock" person for the group. Such persons go the extra mile, remind the others of the meeting, phone everyone to confirm where and when, etc. They simply will not let the group fail by default. If there is no rock person in the group, it is built on sand and will surely fail. The rock person needn't always be the same one or ones.

7. Meet in *equality*. There is to be no domination among us. Leaders will emerge from the group, but they will not be those who dominate. There must be respect for each person's position, even at times of intense disagreement. Remember, it is a dialogue, not a discussion.

8. The pastor, priests, nuns, and members of the pastoral staff are always welcome, but they must come to the meeting not as those with answers, but as fellow searchers. They can be important voices in the group, but they are not to dominate or be looked at as authority figures. When that happens, you have something other than dialogue.

Summary of the Aims or Goals of a Dialogue Group

1. To concretize the Lord's dream, making it possible for members to keep it in focus. Sunday liturgies are just not enough.

2. To discern the "Word of God" and to allow it to form the group into a priestly, kingly, and prophetic people who are *sign* of the Kingdom.

3. To bind up the wounds of those whom the world destroys because they are sign persons, and to give people a place to return to for solace and strength for the continuing battle with our very pagan culture.

4. To be a place where people can answer their needs for community, intimacy, and friendship "in the Lord."

5. To be a place of ongoing Christian formation for its members.

6. To be a support group for "faith" not "religion."

7. To be a place where individual Christians call and are called to ministry in the Lord's service.

A Suggested Format
for Dialogue Groups

If you are among those who have decided to use this book as a basis for group dialogue, you might want to consider the following format for your meetings, if you don't already have one clearly in mind.

1. It is perhaps too burdensome to attempt meeting every week, but that is up to the group. It is suggested that you meet about twice a month.

2. There should be a definite time limit to your meetings. An hour and a half works rather well at first, and two hours should be the maximum, particularly in the beginning.

3. Begin with a short prayer, one that makes it clear that you are meeting in faith, to dialogue in the name of the Lord, and that it is not just a social gathering. Longer shared prayer is a good way to end the meeting.

4. Plan to devote the first 20 to 30 minutes to a Scripture reflection. You may want to use readings of your own choosing, but an easy way to incorporate Scripture dialogue into the meeting is to consider the readings from the upcoming Sunday each time. This has the added advantage of your having shared the readings with your little community, which should make the Sunday liturgy and homily more meaningful.

5. If at first, you don't have much to say, don't worry about it. You'll get better at it. I remember that our group at the beginning, was most uneasy about this part of the meeting and dispensed with the Scripture in five or ten minutes so we could get on to dialoguing on the gut issues. We find now that often we don't get on to the gut issues as such because we bring them all into our reflections on Scripture. And it is not unusual now for our group to spend the whole time relating our experiences to the Scripture readings.

6. Next, turn to the dialogue questions appropriate to that section of the book you are considering. It seems necessary that most, if not all, of those attending the meeting should have read the section of the book about which you are dialoguing *before* you gather. That may not always be possible, but it is an indispensable ideal to strive for. And if most manage to get the job done, then there is no reason for anyone to feel out of place or miss the meeting just because he or she has been unable to do the reading ahead of time. If, on occasion, it should turn out that no one has read it, you might try going round the group having each one read a paragraph or two out loud, stopping to dialogue when the Spirit moves you. Of course, disaster awaits if consistently no one has read it.

7. In processing the dialogue questions, it should be remembered that they are aimed at giving each person in the group the chance to tell his or her story. Take Question 1, and go round the group having each respond. Then Question 2, and so on. The responses should be formed so as not to monopolize the time, but things may come up that require the group to concentrate on them and to give up the planned format for the evening. There is no reason to rush. If the material is not processed at one meeting, it can be held over until the next. It should be noted that there are usually more questions supplied than you can reasonably process in the time allotted. You may want to decide ahead of time which questions look most promising to the group.

8. At the end of the dialogue, the group may feel it appropriate to have some shared prayer, focusing on what has just happened in their dialogue.

9. Finally, the tone of the meeting should be marked as much as possible, by a real sensitivity to everyone present. In our group, for the first two years, two people never uttered a sound. They never missed a meeting. Indeed, they never let us miss a meeting (they were *Peters*), but they never spoke. For them it was very important that they listen to others at that particular moment in their own journeys. Listening was most precious to them. Thank God we didn't ''force'' them to enter the dialogue. Force has no place in such situations. After two years, each began to participate fully in all dialogues, and each has been ''gift'' to the rest of us ever since.

Dialogue Themes

FROM THE APPENDIX

Building a Household Church (1)

1. What does the distinction between *gospel-consumers* and *gospel-creators* mean to you? From your experience, how would *you* describe each of them?

2. From your experience, comment on: "The parish cannot be the basic unit of Church."

3. In your parish what are the *secondary communities* that contribute most to the vitality of the parish? Do these secondary communities have anything in common? What?

4. Sex, family, politics, education, economics and business, and Church are said to be the areas of human life where people are enslaved and in need of liberation.
    a) From your experience, is this true? Explain your position with respect to each of the areas listed above.
    b) Can you think of any other areas where we are generally enslaved and in need of liberation? What are they?

Building a Household Church (2)

1. Does your experience corroborate that "nothing happens unless first a *dream*!"? Give some concrete examples from your experience, one way or the other.

2. How would you express the "dream" of Christianity? Share how that "dream" makes things happen in your life as a Christian.

3. What does it mean to say that people only believe in "incarnation"? Do you believe that is true? Aren't there some other things you believe in?

4. Do you believe in God? (Careful!)

5. From your experience comment on: "All roads lead to Calvary!"

FROM THE INTRODUCTION

1. Do you agree that human experience is revelatory? Give an example from your own life when a profoundly human experience transformed what you believed about God. About the Church.

2. What are your reactions to the claim: "Communally funded experiences should shape our theology, not theology our experience"? Give an example from your own life when theology shaped, or misshaped, your experience.

3. Do you have trouble sharing your thoughts, emotions, and beliefs with others, or are you one of those who finds that easy and helpful? What from your past life, do you think, contributed most to making you the way you are?

4. Are you hungry for someone with whom to share your faith and experiences? Are there others in your area who feel the same way? Any thoughts about how you might get together to answer your common need?

5. How do you feel about lay people gathering in faith to dialogue without a priest being present? Isn't that dangerous?

6. Are you really content with the way the Christian Story is presently being proclaimed to you? If not, what seems to be the problem? What about it disturbs you most?

FROM CHAPTER ONE

The Church as the Bark of Salvation

1. How close does this view of the Church come to what you were taught as a youngster in school?
    a) If you were taught a version of the Bark of Salvation view, what practices of the Church of your youth seem to have been direct consequences of this view? Share some of *your* experiences with those practices.
    b) If you are so young that you were *never* directly taught this view, what vestiges of this approach were still around when you were in school? Did they cause any difficulties or confusions for you?

2. Do any members of your family still hold this view? Does this cause any difficulties in your family? Explain.

3. How prevalent is this view of the Church in your parish? With the priests? With the teachers in the school? With the parishioners in general? Any problems because of this?

4. Perhaps you yourself still hold this view. Do you? If not, when did you give it up? Why? If you do, why do you continue to hold it almost 20 years after Vatican II? What keeps you holding on to it?

5. From *your* perspective, what are the main advantages of the Bark of Salvation view of the Church? The main disadvantages?

6. Some other related themes for possible dialogue might be:
   a) Outside the Church there is no salvation.
   b) Baptism and Eucharist are *in some way* necessary for salvation.
   c) The Catholic community is fragmented primarily because it cannot agree on its understanding of Church.
   d) We need not only Scripture but also a particular vision of Church if we are going to properly discern what is Good News.
   e) The role of priests and laity in the Bark of Salvation.
   f) The status of non-Catholic Christians in this view.
   g) Coping with dissent on board the Bark.

7. Do you think the author's account of this Bark view was accurate? If not, with what do you disagree? Why?

The Church as the Body of Christ

1. Were you ever exposed to the Body of Christ view of the Church in school or religion classes? How close does the version you were taught come to the one given in this chapter? How do they differ? What do you make of that?

2. Were you ever involved in any of the Catholic Action groups? If yes, share some of your better experiences with them with the group. If no, what is or was your attitude toward them? Where did that attitude come from? In retrospect, how valid was it?

3. Share your experience with that classic Catholic remark: Offer it up!

4. Do you now or did you ever think that all salvation comes to the world through the Catholic Church? If so, how do or did you explain how that worked in the case of pagans and primitive peoples who never saw a Christian, much less a Catholic or a missionary?

5. What were your reactions to the Thomas Merton story? To the view that we are called to be co-redeemers with Christ?

6. What are the main advantages to this view over the Bark of Salvation view? What are the main disadvantages?

The Church as the People of God and Sacrament of Salvation

1. What is your perception of Vatican II? How do you feel about it? Did you welcome it or resist it? Why?

2. Go round the group to see if the claim made in the chapter, that those who resisted it were those who remained committed to the old Bark of Salvation view, is verified in your group.

3. If you welcomed Vatican II, what is your reaction to the assessment that it did not go far enough because it attempted a compromise between the Bark of Salvation and Body of Christ views?

4. Of the three views of the Church that have been discussed, which do you prefer? Why?

5. Do you see any advantages to this view over the Body of Christ view? Is it really a step forward? In what ways?

6. What are your reactions to the Council's calling Catholics "the privileged of the privileged"? (Careful! If there is no advantage to being a Catholic over being something else, why be one?)

7. Any reactions to saying that Vatican II is not the last word and that still yet another vision of Christ is aborning? Are you open to yet more change?

The Lesson to Be Learned

1. From your reading of the chapter, what is the lesson to be learned from placing those three visions of the Church side by side? In your view, is it the same lesson the author said he learned, or is it another lesson? Explain.

2. What are your reactions to the claim that the Church is *not* necessary for salvation in any way at all? If that were true, why would one want to remain a Catholic?

3. What difference does it make to say the People of God (Church) is sign but not sacrament of salvation? Evaluate this claim from your own faith and experience.

4. Do you believe God is at work saving *all* of humankind? If so, why do you believe that? What made you come to that conclusion?

5. Why does the author assert that to say that salvation comes to all through the Catholic Church is "slanderous"? Who is slandered, whose reputation is besmirched, if we say that? Where are you in all this?

FROM CHAPTER TWO

Coping With the New Paganism

1. What disturbs you most about the new wave of paganism? How is it manifest in your area or neighborhood? In your own family?

2. Aren't such things as the 700 Club, and other TV evangelisms hopeful signs? What is your attitude toward them?

3. What is your assessment of the effect of Vatican II? Was it helpful or hurtful? Was it, as some say, a mistake? Why? Why not?

4. Do you think a return to the Catholicism of the past would be a positive step in our present predicament? Why? Why not?
    a) If you advocate "going back," to what do you wish to return? Be specific. What practices, teachings, attitudes etc. from the past do you want to recover? Why do you think they would be helpful now?
    b) If you do *not* advocate going back, are you for staying with the *status quo,* or for even more change? How can you justify either alternative in the light of the fact that change seems to have brought on our present predicament?

5. "A return to the past would doom us to live out our faith lives in hypocrisy, publicly professing one thing when our experiences reveal to us another." Do you agree with this assertion? What sorts of experiences have you had which would make "going back" hypocritical? Be specific.

The Fundamentalist Resurgence

1. Do you consider yourself a fundamentalist Christian?
    a) If yes, share with the group the advantages and benefits you

have personally experienced as coming from that.

b) If no, share some experiences in which you encountered fundamentalist Christians. What was or is your reaction to them? What did you admire in them? What did you find difficult to accept?

2. Make a list of "doctrines" or "practices" you associate with fundamentalists. With which do you agree? Disagree? Why?

3. How would *you* describe or define a Christian or Catholic fundamentalist? What is your reaction to the author's claim that a fundamentalist is one who absolutizes something human-made?

4. Have any members of your family been attracted to fundamentalism of late? What attracted them? What problems, if any, has that created for your family?

5. Are there any Bible study groups in your area? Do they tend to be fundamentalist or of a post-Vatican II mindset? Do you belong to such a group? If you do or once did, won't you share what effect it has had on your Christian life?

Scripture (1)

1. The author claims Catholics face a "pastoral crisis" regarding Scripture. Do you have any evidence from your own experience that that is so? Explain.

2. What are your reactions to the following claims?

a) Matthew, Mark, Luke, and John did not themselves write the Gospels.

b) The Gospels are not an account of the life and times of Jesus of Nazareth.

c) Some of the most important of the Pauline epistles were not written by St. Paul.

Does any of that really matter to you? Why? Why not?

3. Is your parish untouched by all this, or are there signs of conflict between the old and new views of Scripture:

a) in the rectory?

b) in the Sunday homilies?

c) in the school?

d) among the people?

What are those signs of conflict and what effect has this had on the parish?

4. Share your thoughts on the following statement: "The Bible is not the Word of God, but it can *become* the Word of God." What in the world does that mean to you?

5. Do you "take offense" at the thought that Scripture may not be as you once learned it was, or are you open to a new understanding of Scripture? What accounts for your openness, if indeed, you are open to the new understanding?

Scripture (2)

1. What are your reactions to the following statement? "What we find in the Bible is not God, but 'God,' which is to say the presence of God *as interpreted by humans* and put into a witnessing narrative account or story."

   a) Even if that statement is true, can you show why it in no way cuts us off from the revelation of God?

   b) If God is not to be found in Scripture, where is he to be found?

2. In your mind, how does the Christian understanding of the Bible differ from Islam's understanding of the Koran?

3. Do you think the Adam and Eve story is literally true? If not, how is it true?

4. What are your reactions to the author's calling the Book of Genesis Israel's *contra-decima* to the world? What does that mean to you?

5. What are your reactions to this book's account of what the Old Testament is about? What the New Testament is about? What does it mean to you to say they "mount a dream"? Why is that important?

6. What does it mean to say that the inspired writers were looking back, but they were *not* writing history? If they weren't writing history, what were they doing?

7. Paul never met Jesus of Nazareth, yet he did encounter the risen Lord on the road to Damascus. What do you make of distinguishing Jesus the Nazarene from the risen Lord? Is there anything significant which the risen Lord can do that Jesus of Nazareth couldn't? What is it, and why is it significant?

8. What are your reactions to the conclusion of this chapter, i.e., that Christians of every age must "get into the process" of revelation and become scribes themselves if they are to really be faithful to their Scriptural heritage?

The Theology of Story

One would like to say that the reason we must search for a more adequate story of God is so that we may have something "life-giving" to hand on to the next generation, which has so consistently rejected the story we were taught in our youth. *But the truth of the matter is otherwise:* It is *we* who have lost our innocence; it is *we* who find we cannot accept the story of God as we originally learned it; it is *we* who have so many unanswered questions. And so it is *we* who must fashion more adequate stories of God *from our own lived experiences.*

1. Have each person *before* the meeting write a paragraph or two presenting his or her story of God from personal experiences. At the meeting, have each read his or her story, making whatever comments of explanation are necessary. Then have the group react to the story. Follow that procedure until all in the group have told their story.

2. *After you have written and shared your own stories,* perhaps you would find it helpful to read and dialogue about the following stories of God, which were produced according to the format above. In what way do you find them "life-giving"?

Story 1: "God is a loving Father and like all loving fathers he gives his children freedom. The children know that the father loves them but they have trouble learning how to respond to that love. They keep searching, making mistakes, and sometimes engage in downright mutiny. Sometimes they love themselves. Sometimes they don't. When they don't love themselves very much, they are sure that God doesn't love them either, and that no one else does. So they say: 'You're right. I'm no damn good. Watch me, I'll prove it to you.' Left alone they reach perfection. Perfect misery, perfect loneliness and perfect isolation. But the Father, loving as he is, gave everybody a family, a faith-filled family which makes it impossible for them to crawl into the hole of self-abasement, self-condemnation, and lifeless isolation. So God became visible in Jesus to counteract the I'm-no-darn-good-anyway syndrome." P.M.

Story 2: "My God is a quiet God. Sometimes I am sure he has no ears and certainly no heart. My God is often hidden from me. My God is not mean, just very quiet. Perhaps he has a blind spot when he encounters me. Perhaps he knows me better than I give him credit for. Perhaps. . .
My God is *me* reaching out to touch, to hold a friend in need. My God is *me* dancing and laughing in celebration of life. My God is *me* struggling to break out, break through—to be known, to be loved, to be accepted
. . . *my God!*" B.B.

Story 3: "God is love. Man tries to love. God is Good. Man basks in his goodness. God just loves man. Man doesn't understand. He tries to please. Please as he will, it is not good enough. Good enough for man, no! Good enough for God, yes! He does not believe. There must be more. I have not done enough, I have not pleased man, I have not pleased my parents, I have not pleased my Church. I have failed. God says, no, I love you as you are. Come home, I have been waiting for you. You are beautiful. *And man believes!*" K.L.

Story 4: "Son, I can't stand it any longer. We've got to keep loving or get out of the God-business. My people complain of how much *they* suffer. Ha! They should trade places with me. I've coddled them, given them all the things they think they can't live without—laws, rites, priests, kings and temples—a definite mistake. No harm in letting them have a 'religion' if it makes them more comfortable with the Joneses. But then they blow me kisses, serve me frozen dinners, and offer to polish my shoes. Give me a pack of honest hostiles any day. At least they're not dull. No choice, Son - we've got to blow it all! We'll show them who's boss and who's servant. Got to get the Word out and make contact. What if they still squirm and sulk? Woo them, Son, woo them. Beg them to try it our way. But leave them free—lay off the flashy power plays. Sure, they may give you the prophet treatment if they get to hating themselves enough. You want me to hedge our bets or something? I said we've got to blow it all! How are you going to endure it? *Like a man,* my Son, *like a man!*" M.Z.

FROM CHAPTER THREE

Religion: The Constant Temptation

1. Are you at peace with the author's distinction between "faith" and "religion"? Or would you prefer, as one priest did, to make the distinction be between "authentic religion" and "inauthentic religion"? Does it really matter what words we use so long as we can agree about what we are talking?

2. What are your reactions to the following:

   a) "Human beings have a *natural* need for religion."

   b) "Religions are human-made."

   c) "Religion is essentially a response to human fear."

   d) "Left to themselves, human beings invariably relate to God religiously."

   e) "Religion dilutes and adulterates faith."

3. Comment on the watchword of religion: "Fear not, trust in God, and he will see to it that none of the things you are afraid of will happen to you." What do you make of the fact that human experience seems to reveal that this just isn't so?

4. As you see it, what consequences follow from saying that religion is based on our belief in God, whereas the Christian faith is based on God's belief in us? Are those consequences desirable? Why? Why not?

5. "We may be surprised and disturbed by just how much 'religion' still exists in each of us . . ." Share some of the "religious" holdovers in your life from which you are still struggling to be free.

6. What "religious" attitudes and practices exist in your parish? How do you feel about them? What changes would you suggest?

The Signs of Religion

1. Go round the group, having each share his or her experiences with reactions to each of the following:
    a) Relating to God out of fear
    b) Feeling the need to appease an angry God
    c) Relating to God out of self-interest, i.e., attempting to get him to do *our* will
    d) Viewing ourselves as little and unworthy in God's sight
    e) Holding that there are two worlds, one in which we live, and another in which God dwells
    f) Holding that some things in the world, e.g., sex, pleasure, etc. are evil in themselves
    g) Violating the freedom and personhood of another by doing physical or psychological harm to her "in the name of the Lord."

The Call to Faith

1) What do you make of each of the following:
    a) "Faith is an ideal presented to humankind by God."
    b) "Faith is a call to intimacy with God."
    c) "Faith is a relationship initiated with the human race for a divine purpose."
    d) "Faith is the most powerful force on earth for transformation, liberty, and love."

2. Comment on the watchword of faith: "Fear not, the things you are afraid of are most likely going to happen to you, but they are not really

the sorts of things that believers ought to be afraid of, and have very little significance compared to transforming the world into the Kingdom.'' What does this mean to you? How does it differ from the watchword of religion?

3. Why does religion come so naturally and easily to us and being people of faith comes so hard? What stands in the way?

4. Have you ever experienced a call to give up religion and move on to faith? If so, won't you share that experience and your understanding of what it means in your own spiritual journey?

5. ''The move from religion to faith requires a radical change in how one views herself, the world, and God.'' Why is that so? Compare religion and faith on how each views:
    a) the self   b) the world   c) God

6. ''The Old Testament is a strange amalgam of faith and religion. The trick is always to know which is which.'' Identify some obviously ''religious'' elements to be found in the Old Testament. Identify some obviously ''faith'' elements. What do you make of that? What norm did you use in labelling each?

7. ''Much of what passes for renewal is actually a reassertion of religiosity, not faith.'' From your own experience, present some examples which either prove or disprove this statement.

8. Doesn't the author go too far when he says: ''The dream of the Lord is frustrated as much by pious religiosity as it is by sin and evil''?

9. What are your reactions to Chapter 3? What in it gave you reason to pause and started you thinking ''new'' thoughts? What in it proved to be most troublesome for you? What proved most helpful?

FROM CHAPTER FOUR

The Adam and Eve I in Each of Us

1. How do you feel about people going for assertiveness training? About women going for such training? Why?

2. Have you ever done any assertiveness training? If so, share how it helped you and how it has altered your self-image. Were there any negative results from the experience? Explain.

3. An ''image of God'' creates and rules a world he or she has made. Share something about the ''world(s)'' you have created and the way

you rule it. Are you completely happy with your "world(s)"? With the way you "rule" it? What changes would you think might improve things?

4. What is the difference between being a work colleague or associate and being a friend? What does it mean to say the former is a "pragmatic" relationship? That the latter is a "deeper" relationship? Any examples from your own life? What makes a relationship deep?

5. From your own experiences compare and evaluate the man-woman relationships:

     a) among teenagers   b) among 20-30 year-olds
     c) among 40-50 year-olds   d) among the elderly

In which group are women most accepted as equal? As subservient? What accounts for this?

6. What does the following statement mean to you? "There is nothing particularly redeeming about the Adam and Eve I relationship."

7. What is your reaction to this Jewish interpretation of Chapter 1 of Genesis? Did it help or confuse you? Explain.

The Adam and Eve II in Each of Us

1. "Redemptiveness is not achieved by the forward surges of Adam and Eve I, but by yielding to the other Adam and Eve II style." What does that line mean to you? According to your experience is it true? Explain.

2. "Our strengths divide us; it is in our weakness that we are one." What evidence do you have from your own experiences for the truth of that statement? If it is true, what does that tell us about how to relate to one another? How did the Lord relate to people?

3. Share an Adam and Eve II experience when you felt called not to assert your will or your rights but "to be servant." What were the results? On yourself? On others?

4. When do you feel most lonely and isolated in your life? If community and friendship are "gifts" which can't be earned, does that mean I can't do anything about loneliness? Must I, like Adam II, simply wait to be gifted?

5. "Adam and Eve II crave personal (not necessarily sexual) intimacy." What does that mean to you?

6. Does your experience verify that real intimacy involves three persons—I, Thou, and He—because it is always a gift from the Lord God?

7. Compare the God of Adam and Eve I with the God of Adam and Eve II. What would it mean to say that the former is a religious God, and the latter the God of faith?

Time I and Time II

1. Do you have an experience of there being two kinds of time, or is it all the same to you? What do you make of the author's twofold division of time?

2. How would you describe Time II? Give some examples from your own life.

3. What does it mean to say that Time I can be lost or wasted but that Time II cannot. Does that make any sense to you? Explain.

4. Take a sheet of paper and chart a typical day showing how you spent your time. Identify what you did as a) Time I—work, b) Time I—wasted, c) Time II—alone time, d) Time II—relationship building. Then have each one share his or her chart with the group, saying whether they are satisfied with their use of time, what they would like to change, and what is the greatest obstacle to that change.

FROM CHAPTER FIVE

Our Story

1. What is your reaction to *Our Story?* What do you find especially helpful in it? What do you find troublesome?

2. Comment on the following criticisms made of this proclamation. If you disagree with the criticism, say how *you* would answer it.
   a) Abraham seems more important than Christ.
   b) It seems to ignore that God is transcendent.
   c) It is actually against the faith to say that God is, and always was, "human." That's sacrilege!
   d) The crucifixion which is central to Christianity is mentioned only in passing.
   e) None of the Sacraments of Salvation are mentioned.
   f) Being a Christian doesn't seem important when God is described as the God-with-all-his-people.

3. Are there any other criticisms which *you* would like to make?

4. Is there any sense in which this could be called a "salvation" story? What would "salvation" mean in that case?

5. From what has been said in the preceding sections of this book, why is this a proclamation of "faith"? On the basis of *Our Story,* how would you describe "faith"?

Our Faith

For each of the seven articles of the "creed" do the following: Have someone in the group read the article out loud. Then have each share his or her reactions to the article, showing why it is truly an article of "faith" and what the "religious" version of the same article would look like.

Themes for Dialogue Arising from the Proclamation

1. What say you of Jesus? See *Our Story* (OS), 5-6; *Our Faith* (OF), 3.)

2. What does it mean to worship God? (See OS, 4.)

3. How can we deny the "Monster God" and still hold out for hell fire damnation? (See OF, 1 & 6.)

4. What does it mean to be a sign-people? (See OS, 3-4; OF, 4.)

5. If Abraham was willing to kill Isaac, doesn't that prove that he is not a person of faith, but is "religious"? (See OS, 1.)

6. Is our God really a God of Freedom? (See OS, 4; OF, 6.)

7. Is being a person of faith easier for the poor or the rich and powerful? Or is it the same for all? (See OS, 10.)

8. What do we mean by the Kingdom? (See OF, 3, 4, 5.)

9. How does God's forgiveness come to us humans? (See OF, 6.)

10. Is the dream of the Lord really opposed to the American Dream?

FROM CHAPTER SIX

The Exodus Experience

1. Elizabeth O'Connor claims, "We are the people of the Exodus." But are we? What is it like in your parish?

2. Share an Exodus experience from your own life. What is it about that experience that leads you to call it an Exodus experience? What are the essential marks of Exodus?

3. From your own lived experience comment on the truth of Feuerbach's remark: "What was once good claims to be good for all times."

4. Comment on the following:
    a) "The long trek out of bondage is not over."
    b) "If something new comes into being in us . . . something old has had to make way for it."
    c) "The temptation is *always*—to go back!"
    d) "Each time we break camp the issue is once again in doubt."
    e) "We resist change, even when it is liberating."

5. Make a list of the major obstacles to "Exodus." Then share your list with the group.

Our Lost Spirituality

1. Do you agree that adult Catholics are generally suffering pain from the loss of their spirituality? What are the signs? Where are you in all this?

2. Compare your "spiritual life" of today to what it was about ten years ago. Has it improved or worsened? How do you feel about that? What are the major differences you detect? What caused them?

3. Do you feel that going back to the "spirituality" of your youth would be a life-giving experience for you? Why? Why not? Have *you* ever tried to do so? Share what happened.

4. What are your reactions to the two definitions of spirituality in this chapter?
    a) "A spirituality of faith is a patterned style of behavior whereby we seek to put and maintain ourselves in touch with God by relating to him in intimacy."
    b) "Spirituality is our attempt at an altered state of consciousness wherein we come to *see* the normally invisible and *hear* the normally inaudible dimensions of life."
Which of the definitions do you prefer? Why? Could you, perhaps, suggest another and better one?

5. Comment on the following:
    a) "There is, generally, no going home again."
    b) "Praise the Lord, isn't something I say; it is something I *am!*

c) "Spirituality is not a matter of religious practices; it is a matter of living a certain kind of life."

6. What does your experience reveal to you about the following statement: "If we have learned anything in the past decades, it is that we cannot go on indefinitely without an identifiable spirituality." That can't be true, can it? Many Catholics seem to get along just fine without one.

7. Evaluate the "spiritual lives" of your children. Do they even have a spiritual life? Where are they with regard to Sunday Mass? The parish? The Lord God?

8. What were your reactions to the author's account of what turned him on as a father, and his application of that to God?

9. If we give up or have given up the religious practices of the past, how are we to distinguish our present state from laxity or indifference?

Prayer

1. When we say we feel "the need to pray," of what, exactly, do we feel the need? Can we distinguish that need from some other recognizable human needs, such as the need:
   a) to be alone
   b) to move back and away from the hectic pace of our lives
   c) to get our minds off our troubles
   d) to "do something constructive" in situations in which we are otherwise powerless
How do you see the "need to pray" as different from these?

2. What are your reactions to each of the following contradictory assessments of the situation?
   a) "The gravest sin against religion is not to understand or recognize our total and essential dependence on God. It is forgetting, neglecting and practically denying that we are creatures and that God is God. Another sin against religion is not to pray anymore. Such Christians do not deny the necessity of prayer. Nor do they pose the question of its efficacy. But they no longer pray. Or they pray only rarely" (Gustav Thils, *Christian Holiness*, Lannoo, 1961).
   b) "The cosmic drama, notwithstanding its grandeur and splendour, no matter how distinctly it reflects the image of Creation, cannot provoke man to prayer. Of course it may arouse an adoring-ecstatic mood in man; it may even inspire man to raise his voice in a song of praise and thanksgiving. Nevertheless, ecstatic

adoration, even if expressed in a hymn, is not prayer. Prayer transcends the bounds of worship and must not be reduced to its external-technical aspects, such as praise, thanksgiving and petition" (Joseph Soloveitchik, *The Lonely Man of Faith*, 1965).

c) "Some people still feel guilty because they do not pray the way they once did. We should be grateful that so many people have been freed from the ghosts of obsessive praying. Those who have urged the constant repetition of certain prayers so that each moment is filled with something that sounds like prayer have merely activated obsessive mechanisms in man. The truth is that people pray more than they think and better than they imagine" (Eugene Kennedy, *A Contemporary Meditation on Prayer*, Thomas More, 1975).

3. "There are men and women who throw their energies into efforts to pray their way into life. The truth, of course, is that *we live our way into*

Our Flight From Intimacy

1. If "confrontation" is touching and being touched by someone only superficially, and "encounter" is touching and being touched by someone profoundly, give some examples from your life when you settled for the former when the latter was clearly called for.

2. What was your reaction to the following statement: "Without encounter all spiritualities would inevitably be reduced to nothing more than religious confrontations, confrontations in which God would try to subject us to his will, or what is equally comic, we would attempt to bend him to ours."

3. How can one complain that so much of traditional spirituality is merely "religious confrontation"? Doesn't God want us subject to his will? That's the norm for holiness, isn't it?

4. How do you understand what the author calls "salvation time"? How do Time I and Time II differ? Why can only Time II not be lost or wasted?

5. Comment on: "Nuts, it's time for our group to meet for dialogue and faith sharing *again*."

Our Lack of Vision

1. Things are not what they seem. True. But happily life reveals its ironic nature to us if we but live long enough. Unfortunately this

revelation occurs, if at all, only after the mistakes of youth. What do you see clearly now that you wish you had seen earlier in your life:

a) about God?   b) about humankind?
c) about the Church?   d) about sexuality?
e) about marriage?   f) about yourself?
g) about parenthood?   h) other?

2. "If things were simply as they appear, humankind would have no need of spirituality." Suppose that life were exactly as it appears and that we knew that to be the case, what would life be like? Why would a spirituality not be needed?

3. Are you presently satisfied that you now see reality clearly enough? *prayer."* What does this remark of Eugene Kennedy mean to you? Do you know people who try to pray their way into life? What are they like? What does it mean to "live your way into prayer"? What are the people who do that like?

4. Comment on the following: "God does not settle for poses, affectations or fine but insincere words. *He invites us to be persons in his presence.* A mature prayer life takes this seriously."

5. How do you interpret and understand the three levels of prayer? Especially the distinction between *religious prayer* and *the prayer of faith?*

6. From your own experience share your most satisfying prayer experience. What made it so satisfactory?

FROM CHAPTER SEVEN

Human Intimacy

"Personal intimacy requires me to be able to disappear from the world as an object of competition, rivalry and comparison, so as to feel my solidarity with people in their brokenness" (Henri Nouwen).

1. The author claims that at times we have all had an irresistible urge to reveal ourselves in our brokenness to someone, to anyone. What evidence, if any, do you have from your own experience that we crave "intimacy" as so defined?

2. Share an experience in which you had the urge to reveal yourself, your *real* self, to someone close to you. If you had the courage to do so, was the experience "redemptive"? Why? Why not?

3. What does the following remark mean to you? "Our strengths divide and isolate us; it is in our weaknesses that we are one."
   a) Apply this to husband-wife relationships
   b) To personal friendships
   c) To work or task (Adam and Eve I) relationships

4. From your experience, is genital sexuality a help or a hindrance to genuine intimacy? Explain.

5. Is consecrated virginity or celibacy a help or hindrance to intimacy? Explain.

6. What were your reactions to the following assertion? "There is no use any longer in our pretending to love everyone in general (Christian charity) if we are not willing to be intimate with someone in particular." Could a person practice Christian charity and still avoid intimacy with another human person? How do you feel about those who claim that the only intimacy they require is "with God"?

7. Comment on the following remark: "Marriages and friendships that fail to achieve intimacy are doomed to disintegrate or to be superficially continued out of habit or self-interest."
How does this relate to the current epidemic of divorces?

8. From the perspective of "intimacy," evaluate your own personal stand on each of the following:
   a) ERA or Women's Liberation
   b) The Ordination of Women
   c) Parenthood
   d) Men and women living together without being married.

Obstacles to Intimacy

1. From your experience, what would you say are the greatest obstacles to intimacy?

2. In what order would you rank the following obstacles to intimacy?
   a) Pride
   b) Being a "religious" Christian
   c) Fear
   d) The "machismo" myth for males
   e) Lust
   f) Selfishness
   g) The American ideal of rivalry and competition
   h) The new "assertiveness" of women
   i) Ignorance that "intimacy" is a human imperative

3. Comment on: "We exist with one another armed to the teeth, therefore the first step toward intimacy is disarmament, or at least the

pledge not to use our defensive weapons against the other.''
Isn't that an unrealistic ideal? What would happen if we disarmed ourselves in our personal relations? Wouldn't people walk all over us? How do you feel about that?

4. Share an incident from your own experience when you fired off your defensive ''missiles'' at another, and lived to regret it. What lesson is to be learned from your experience?

5. Share an experience in which you were on the receiving end of salvos from someone you really love. What effect did it have on your relationship? Was the damage done permanent? If not, what did you do to repair that damage?

6) What is your opinion of the claim that we all ''make book'' on one another and that this is automatic? Many claim that this is not true. It is hard to conceive of Pope John XXIII or Mother Teresa of Calcutta doing that. Do people like that learn to not ''fire their missiles,'' or do you think they advance so far in walking with the Lord that they even manage to stop ''making book'' altogether?

Joy

1. ''In truth, I know not why I am so glad, it heartens me and joys my heart. Yet how I caught it, found it or came to it, of what stuff it is made or where it came from, I cannot say. But this I know. I have never been so joyed, never so whole, never so much in touch with what is truly good.'' Have you ever felt that way? Describe the situation. Be specific.

2. From your own experience, is it true that we really get more joy from persons than from things? Compare how you felt in the experience you shared in 1 above with how you felt when you got a new stereo, a new car, or bought your house.

3. Comment on: ''The mystery of redemptive joy does not come from 'having' so much as from 'giving.' '' Could a consumer generation become so jaded that the reverse would be true for them?

4. ''Things can be very good, but from the point of view of faith only persons can be the dwelling place of Goodness Itself.'' Any reactions to that?

5. Answer the following question and explain your answer. ''Yes or no, is there any joy equal to the joy of really caring for another, or forgetting, forgetting, or affirming, and loving?''

Redemption

1. Comment on: "If intimacy is not redemptive, then nothing in this life ever can be."
   a) What makes something "redemptive"?
   b) What is it about intimacy that makes it redemptive?

2. "Redemption is just another name for learning the lessons of intimacy. Many *never* learn them."
   a) From your own experiences, what lessons have the moments of authentic intimacy (Time II) taught you?
   b) What persons, places, things, situations, attitudes, etc. present you with the greatest obstacles to learning what intimacy has to reveal?
   c) In your judgment, why do so many among us *never* learn those lessons?

3. Why does the author say that merely "keeping the commandments" is insipid, i.e. tasteless? Could one keep the commandments and still not learn the redemptive lessons of intimacy? Explain.

4. What do you understand by the claim that life's central lesson is learning to "let go" or to "yield"? Could I keep all the commandments and still not learn those lessons? Explain.

5. What does the word "incarnation" mean to you after reading this chapter? If it refers to something we also experience and not just something found in Jesus, what is the significance of "incarnation" with respect to salvation or redemption?

6. Comment on: "Most Protestants think that Christianity is basically a morality play. The Catholic tradition seems to place more stress on its being a divinization process."
   a) From your experience, is that statement true? Aren't there just as many Catholics who view Christianity as a morality play? Are you one of them?
   b) What difference does it make how we view Christianity? What advantages are there to seeing it as a divinization process rather than a morality play?

The Crucifixion

1. Have someone in the group read Walter Imbiorski's account out loud.
   a) What are your reactions to it as you hear it read to you?

b) What were your reactions when you first read it yourself? Has there been any change in your reactions?

c) Are or were you offended by this "caricature"? Why? Why not?

2. Since we all learned as children, that we were saved by the shedding of Christ's blood, we were not at first offended by that fact. Now in adult life, do you feel any differently about it? Explain.

3. What is your reaction to the author's hypothesis that we were not redeemed by the Good Friday event? Isn't that unorthodox?

4. What sense do you make of the claim that we were redeemed more by the "incarnation" than by the "crucifixion"?

5. How would *you* tell the salvation story? What is it that redeems us?

6. Comment on the following:

a) Yahweh forbade all human sacrifice.

b) Jesus died because he was human.

c) The Old Testament prophecies don't make the murder of Jesus necessary for salvation.

d) Christians have not always held that we were redeemed by the crucifixion.

e) The murder of Jesus was exclusively and fully willed by his enemies, not by himself or his Father.

Intimacy With God

"I prostrated myself, and then I heard a voice speaking. It said, 'Son of man, *stand up* so that I, the Lord Yahweh, may speak to you' " (Ezechiel 2:1).

1. Intimacy with the God of power and might is really impossible. Any comments? Why is this true? Or not true?

2. From your own experiences, tell of the times you have felt being:

a) far from God   b) in fear of God

c) close to God   d) free in his presence

3. What reasons can you give for the fact that genuine human intimacy always leads to God, i.e., always involves I—Thou—He?

4. Are you comfortable with the thought of relating to God in *freedom, reciprocity,* and *equality*? Doesn't relating to God in equality lead to idolatry of the human?

5. If intimacy rests on weakness, what do you make of God's passionate desire to be intimate with humankind? That surely is ironic!

6. What do you make of Soren Kierkegaard's statement given at the beginning of the chapter? Does that mean that a young person can't come to know the truth of God's intimate presence?

FROM CHAPTER EIGHT

Sin

1. How do you define sin? What is its distinguishing characteristic? What has to be present in an action to make it a sin? What has to be missing?

2. Evaluate the following definitions of sin:
   a) Sin is breaking God's commandments.
   b) Sin is doing something willfully and maliciously to harm another.
   c) Sin is failing to do what love requires in any given situation.

3. "Sin can become a tradition, and like all traditions it gives life a definite direction." What does it mean to you to say sin can become a tradition?

4. Sin moves life *inward,* i.e., away from intimacy with the other (be it God or a person). Sin moves life *backward,* i.e., away from the Kingdom which is coming. Sin moves life *deathward,* i.e., away from what is life-giving.
Identify some situations from your life, the life of your neighborhood, the life of your parish, in which you judge that sin has become something of a "tradition."

5. Comment on each of the following:
   a) "Because we recognize the inward, backward, deathward direction of sin in our own lives, we feel like hypocrites unworthy to walk with the Lord."
   b) "The Christian community (Church) attempts to give life the direction Jesus gave it, that is, outward toward redemptive intimacy, forward toward the Kingdom, and lifeward toward resurrection."

Irony and Parables

1. The author says that there are three classes of people: (1) those who take life for what it is worth on the surface, (2) those who suspect that there is more to life than meets the eye, (3) those who can't make up their minds and vacillate between the other positions, as the occasion demands.

a) Describe the lifestyle of those you know who are in the first group. The second group. The third group.
b) Which group are you in? Are you satisfied with being there? Why? Why not?

2. "Human life is either *absurd* or *ironic.*" What does that statement mean to you? (Hint: Take *absurd* to indicate that life has no ultimate meaning. Take *ironic* to indicate that life has an ultimate meaning, but it is not what it appears to be.)

3. "When the disciples got near him, they asked: 'Why do you speak in parables?' He answered, 'I use parables when I speak because people look but do not see, they listen but do not understand'' (Matt. 13:10, 13). In the light of this text, comment on the following:
a) "Jesus is the *Parable of God.*"
b) "Jesus is not quite what he appeared to be—and neither are we."
c) "Parables are ironic invitations to intimacy."

4. Take two or three of the group's favorite parables from the Gospels and dialogue about them, trying to see if you can find the "irony" in them.

5. Comment on: "The loss of intimacy always begins with our inability to see the Lord, each other, and ourselves with sufficient irony."

Walking With the Lord
1. The author claims that to "walk with the Lord" is to have the same effect on people that he did. What was that effect?
a) If that is the norm, are you "walking with the Lord"?
b) What about the seemingly good Christian who have just the opposite effect on people? What do you make of that? And of the fact that there seems to be so many Christians of that sort? It it "faith" vs. "religion" once again?

2. Why is it important that we affirm the other? Psychologically? From a faith perspective?

3. Share your reactions to Pope John XXIII. To Martin Luther King, Jr. To Mother Teresa. Are they as great as the author suggests? Does Martin Luther King, Jr. really belong in that group?

4. Can you distinguish the differences within yourself and in the effects on others when you act out of your gifts, rather than out of your needs and compulsions? What are the differences? What do they tell you about life? About faith?

5. "We learn of our gifts from the smiles, joyful songs, and feelings of enhancement we discern in others when we act. They reveal our truest selves to us." Share from your experience when this has happened.

6. "Were it not for the experiences of gracing and being graced by others, we would miss the 'gift-dimension' of life and never see reality ironically enough."
   a) Does life have a "gift-dimension"? Explain.
   b) What does it mean "to grace" and "be graced"? Any examples? I thought only God did that!

7. What is your overall reaction to this chapter? What in it did you find most illuminating and helpful? What most troublesome?

FROM CHAPTER NINE
Knowledge of God
1. What do you take "knowledge of God" to mean in the scriptural montage presented by the author? What were your reactions to it?

2. What is the difference between "knowing God" and "knowing about God"?
   a) Make a list of some of the more important things you know "about" God.
   b) As best you can, describe in words an experience in which you are now confident you came to know God.

3. How do 2a and 2b above differ?

4. "Knowledge of God must be allowed 'to happen to us'; it must be accepted as gift." What are your reactions to this statement?

5. Comment on the following remark of Alan Watts: "There are a million methods for expressing knowledge and love of God, but not one for attaining it. And yet the thing happens—God is known and God is loved."
   a) Why does "the thing happen," if it can't be achieved?
   b) How did it happen to you?

6. "Much of what 'religious' Christians say about God amounts to nothing short of slander against the Father." Do you agree? If so, then share some of the more outrageous slanders against the Father you have personally heard Christians make. What were your reactions?

7. Each of the following one-liners represents an attempt by Irene Dugan to share her experience of God. What do you make of these

statements? How would you translate them? What one-liners would you add that have come from your own experience?

   a) "He is busy in us—but we don't even give him recognition."
   b) "We need to stop—to allow awareness of him to happen."
   c) "To know God—is really to know myself."
   d) "He is *parent!*"
   e) "In relations with others, we have to be like God. Wait and pray, but without anxiety."
   f) "Be at peace—let things be."
   g) "When one knows God, one gives off peace."

8. "We cannot say the right things about God unless we have had a God-experience of Adam and Eve II." What does this statement mean to you? Is it true?

9. "Nothing betrays us and reveals that we do not really *know him* more than the way we cope with failure. We Catholics have made a real botch of that." Show how this is true in your own life. In the life of your parish. In the life of your community.

10. Comment on the following: "Those who demand, oppress, wound, condemn, and punish in the name of the Lord show that they don't really know him." What are your reactions to this statement? Does it make authority worthless or unimportant? Or does it mean that "real" authority works otherwise? Explain.

The Manufactured God

1. "Man is always trying to manufacture God, or a sense of God and therefore ignores the one that is actually given, because there is no credit to be gained in accepting a gift." From your own experiences with people comment on this remark of Alan Watts.

2. How do you react to the author's claim that "the 'religious' version of how God works in the world seems to me to be taking the name of the Lord in vain"?

3. According to this chapter, it is the "manufactured God" who threatens, visits wrath, demands affirmation, puts conditions on his gifts, saves only Christians, wills that we suffer, delights in the law, and is satisfied if we but keep the commandments.

   a) What are your reactions to this?
   b) Why is this the "antithesis of the God of faith"?

4. How would you suggest one go about discerning whether a person knows God or only a "manufactured" god? What are the telltale signs of the latter?

Unselfing

1. Do you agree with Iris Murdoch that "human beings are naturally selfish" and that "the psyche relentlessly looks after itself"? Explain.

2. How do you react to the claim that "the self, the place where we live, is a place of illusion so we do not necessarily see what confronts us"? Apply this to our "knowledge of God."

3. Comment on the following:
   a) "So filled with the self are we that we can't quite be sure that what we know is reality."
   b) "Two defense mechanisms the self uses to protect itself from pain are: (1) to inflate the self, (2) to invent theological fictions."
   c) "Unselfing is the primary goal of any authentic spirituality."

4. Do you think unselfing is an important ingredient of a human life? If so, why is it important? How did you come to learn this lesson?

5. What are the most effective mechanisms of unselfing in your own life? Do you find that they enrich or impoverish your life? Explain.

6. What effect has unselfing had on the quality of your life? In relation to others? In helping you come to know God?

Abba-Amen

1. What does it mean to you to say that God is Abba or our Father? What does that tell you about how he relates to us? About how we should relate to him?

2. "The heart of Jesus' Abba-experience is that all have reason to hope. *Redemptive intimacy is available to all.*" What are your reactions to this? What about hardened sinners?

3. What is the author trying to say when he claims: "Because God is Father, we are called to say and to live 'Amen' "? Why does God's being Father mean that we must not only say but live *let it be?*

4. "God deals with us as a *present but waiting God.*" Does your own experience verify this claim? Explain.

5. Why do we feel we've got to badger and threaten ourselves and others into being good? Why can't we let others be?

6. If a major task of Church is to proclaim God to the world, and if we are Church, then what is to be our proclamation of God?

BIBLIOGRAPHY

BOOKS

Baum, Gregory. *Man Becoming*. New York: Herder & Herder, 1970.
Becker, Ernest. *The Denial of Death*. New York: Free Press, 1973.
Evely, Louis. *If the Church Is To Survive*. New York: Doubleday, 1972.
Fox, Matthew. *On Becoming A Musical Mystical Bear*. New York: Harper & Row, 1972.
Howe, Reuel. *The Miracle of Dialogue*. New York: Seabury Press, 1963.
The Jerome Biblical Commentary. Englewood Cliffs, N.J.: Prentice Hall, 1968.
Kennedy, Eugene. *A Contemporary Mediation on Prayer*. Chicago: Thomas More, 1975.
Kung, Hans. *On Being A Christian*. New York: Doubleday, 1976.
Mayeroff, Milton. *On Caring*. New York: Harper & Row, 1971.
McKuen, Elizabeth. "New Directions In Theology: The Theology of Story." Unpublished Address before U.S. Bishops' Committee on the Laity, April 14, 1978.
Murdoch, Iris. *The Sovereignty of Good*. New York: Schocken, 1971.
New American Bible. New York: P.J. Kenedy & Sons, 1970.
© Confraternity of Christian Doctrine, Washington, D.C.
Nouwen, Henri. *Intimacy*. Notre Dame, Ind.: Fides Press, 1969.
O'Connor, Elizabeth. *The New Community*. New York: Harper & Row, 1976.
Schillebeeckx, Edward. *Jesus: An Experiment in Christology*. New York: Seabury Press, 1979.
Shea, John. *What A Modern Catholic Believes About Sin*. Chicago: Thomas More, 1971.
_____. *The Challenge of Jesus*. Chicago: Thomas More, 1975.
_____. *Stories of God*. Chicago: Thomas More, 1978.
_____. *Stories of Faith*. Chicago: Thomas More, 1980.
Soloveitchik, Joseph. "The Lonely Man of Faith," *Tradition,* VII, 2 (1965), pp. 5-67.
Thils, Gustav. *Christian Holiness*. Lannoo, Belgium, 1961.
Watts, Alan. *Behold The Spirit*. New York: Random House, 1971.
Weber, Max. *Sociology of Religion*. Boston: Beacon Press, 1964.

ECCLESIAL DOCUMENTS
  1) Encyclicals of Pius XII:
     Divino Afflante Spiritu, N.C.W.C. ed., 1943.
     Mystici Corporis Christi, N.C.W.C. ed., 1943.
  2) Pontifical Biblical Commission Report:
     "On The Historicity of The Gospels." *Catholic Biblical Quarterly,* XXVI (1964), pp. 299-312.
  3) Vatican II Documents:
     Dogmatic Constitution on the Church, (Lumen Gentium), Nov. 21, 1964, in *The Documents of Vatican II,* ed. Walter Abbott, S.J., 1966, pp. 14-96.
     Dogmatic Constitution on Divine Revelation, (Dei Verbum), Nov. 18, 1965. Abbott edition, pp. 111-128.
     Pastoral Constitution on the Church in the Modern World, (Gaudium et Spes), Dec. 7, 1965, Abbott edition, pp. 199-308.
     Decree on the Church's Missionary Activity, (Ad Gentes), Dec. 7, 1965, Abbott edition, pp. 584-630.